First World War
and Army of Occupation
War Diary
France, Belgium and Germany

59 DIVISION
177 Infantry Brigade
Lincolnshire Regiment
2/5 Battalion
1 January 1916 - 31 July 1918

WO95/3023/3

The Naval & Military Press Ltd
www.nmarchive.com
Published in association with The National Archives

Published by

The Naval & Military Press Ltd

Unit 10 Ridgewood Industrial Park,

Uckfield, East Sussex,

TN22 5QE England

Tel: +44 (0) 1825 749494

www.naval-military-press.com

www.nmarchive.com

This diary has been reprinted in facsimile from the original. Any imperfections are inevitably reproduced and the quality may fall short of modern type and cartographic standards.

© **Crown Copyright**
Images reproduced by permission of The National Archives, London, England, 2015.

Contents

Document type	Place/Title	Date From	Date To
Heading	2-5th Bn Lincoln Regt Feb 1917-July 1918 And 1916 Jan & Feb		
Heading	WO95/3023/3 2/5 Battalion Lincolnshire Regiment		
Heading	War Diary Of 2/5 Lincolnshire Regt. From January 1st 1916 To January 31st 1916		
War Diary	Harpenden	01/01/1916	31/01/1916
Heading	War Diary Of 2/5 Lincolnshire Regt From 31/1/16 To 22/2/1916		
War Diary	Harpenden	31/01/1916	22/02/1916
Heading	WO95/3023/4 2/5 Battalion Lincolnshire Regiment		
War Diary	Fovant	23/02/1917	23/02/1917
War Diary	Southampton	23/02/1917	23/02/1917
War Diary	Le Havre	24/02/1917	24/02/1917
War Diary	Le Saleux	25/02/1917	25/02/1917
War Diary	Bacovel	25/02/1917	27/02/1917
War Diary	Fouencamps	27/02/1917	28/02/1917
Operation(al) Order(s)	2/5 Lincoln Regt Order No 1	26/02/1917	26/02/1917
Operation(al) Order(s)	2/5 Lincoln Rgt Order No 2	27/02/1917	27/02/1917
War Diary	Bayonvillers	01/03/1917	06/03/1917
War Diary	Triangle Copse	07/03/1917	07/03/1917
War Diary	Trenches Front Line	07/03/1917	07/03/1917
War Diary	Front Line Trenches	08/03/1917	12/03/1917
War Diary	Triangle Wood	13/03/1917	18/03/1917
War Diary	Trenches	19/03/1917	21/03/1917
War Diary	Foucaucourt	22/03/1917	25/03/1917
War Diary	Eterpigny	25/03/1917	26/03/1917
War Diary	Beaumetz	26/03/1917	27/03/1917
War Diary	Nobescourt Farm	27/03/1917	31/03/1917
Operation(al) Order(s)	177th Infantry Brigade Operation Order No 1	04/03/1917	04/03/1917
Miscellaneous	March Table Issued The 177th Infantry Brigade Operation No.1	01/03/1917	01/03/1917
Miscellaneous	March Table 2		
Miscellaneous	Amendment To 177th Infantry Brigade Operation Order No. 1	04/03/1917	04/03/1917
Operation(al) Order(s)	177th Infantry Brigade Operation Order No 3	10/03/1917	10/03/1917
Operation(al) Order(s)	Operation Order No. 12 Appendix XIV	19/04/1917	19/04/1917
Operation(al) Order(s)	Lincoln Regt Operation Order No. 13	28/04/1917	28/04/1917
Heading	War Diary Of 2/5 Bn The Lincolnshire Regt. From 1st April 1917 To 30th April 1917		
War Diary	Nobescourt Farm	01/04/1917	05/04/1917
War Diary	Roisel	06/04/1917	09/04/1917
War Diary	Templeux	09/04/1917	09/04/1917
War Diary	Hargicourt	09/04/1917	19/04/1917
War Diary	Vraignes	20/04/1917	28/04/1917
War Diary	Le. Verguier	28/04/1917	30/04/1917
Miscellaneous	Appendix 13	13/04/1917	13/04/1917
Heading	War Diary Of 2/5 Bn Lincolnshire Regt. From 1/5/17 To 31/5/17		
War Diary	Le. Verguier	01/05/1917	06/05/1917
War Diary	Jeancourt	07/05/1917	15/05/1917

War Diary	Cartigny	16/05/1917	25/05/1917
War Diary	Equancourt	26/05/1917	27/05/1917
War Diary	Gouzeaucourt Wood	27/05/1917	30/05/1917
War Diary	Beaucamp	31/05/1917	31/05/1917
Heading	War Diary Of The 2/5th Bn Lincolnshire Regt. From 1/6/17 To 30/6/17		
War Diary	Beaucamp	01/06/1917	07/06/1917
War Diary	Gouzeaucourt Wood	08/06/1917	17/06/1917
War Diary	Beaucamp	18/06/1917	21/06/1917
War Diary	Equancourt	22/06/1917	30/06/1917
Miscellaneous	2/5th Lincolnshire Regt Defence Scheme for Support Battalion	10/06/1917	10/06/1917
Heading	War Diary Of 2/5th Bn Lincolnshire Regt. From 1st July 1917 To 31st July 1917		
War Diary	Neuville	01/07/1917	05/07/1917
War Diary	Beaucamp	06/07/1917	10/07/1917
War Diary	Barastre	11/07/1917	31/07/1917
Heading	War Diary Of The 2/5th Lincolnshire Regt. From 1/8/17 To 31/8/17		
War Diary	Barastre (o.16.a)	01/08/1917	22/08/1917
War Diary	Hedauville (9.34.c)	22/08/1917	30/08/1917
War Diary	Briele (j.10.b)	31/08/1917	31/08/1917
Heading	War Diary Of The 2/5th Battn Lincolnshire Regt From 1/9/17 To 30/9/17		
War Diary	Winnezeele	01/09/1917	20/09/1917
War Diary	Hilhoek (L.15b.4.6) Sheet 27	21/09/1917	23/09/1917
War Diary	Goldfish Chateau H.11 Central Sheet 28	23/09/1917	24/09/1917
War Diary	St. Jean (C.27.d) Sheet 28	24/09/1917	25/09/1917
War Diary	W Of Hill 37	26/09/1917	27/09/1917
War Diary	E Of Hill 37 (D.20.a)	27/09/1917	27/09/1917
War Diary	Bank Farm	28/09/1917	29/09/1917
War Diary	Derby Camp (H.1a Central) Sheet 28	30/09/1917	30/09/1917
Operation(al) Order(s)	177th Infantry Brigade Operation Order No. 50	24/09/1917	24/09/1917
Map	Map		
Miscellaneous	Account Of The Action By The 2/5th Lincolnshire Regiment	03/10/1917	03/10/1917
Diagram etc	Attack Formation Of 2/5th Bn Lincolnshire Regt		
Map	Map		
Heading	War Diary Of 2/5th Battalion The Lincolnshire Regiment From 1/10/17 To 31/10/17		
War Diary	Poperinghe	01/10/1917	02/10/1917
War Diary	Bas Hamel	02/10/1917	06/10/1917
War Diary	Lugy	06/10/1917	10/10/1917
War Diary	Pressy-Les-Pernes	11/10/1917	11/10/1917
War Diary	Divion	12/10/1917	13/10/1917
War Diary	Souchez	13/10/1917	13/10/1917
War Diary	Avion	14/10/1917	17/10/1917
War Diary	Givenchy (S.10. A Y C)	18/10/1917	21/10/1917
War Diary	Souchez (36c.SW)	22/10/1917	29/10/1917
War Diary	Lens	29/10/1917	31/10/1917
Heading	War Diary Of The 2/5th Battalion The Lincolnshire Regiment From 1st To 30th November 1917		
War Diary	Lens	01/11/1917	06/11/1917
War Diary	Cite De Rollencourt	07/11/1917	13/11/1917
War Diary	Grand Servins	13/11/1917	17/11/1917
War Diary	Wanquetin	18/11/1917	19/11/1917

War Diary	Bellacourt	20/11/1917	21/11/1917
War Diary	Achiet-Le-Petit	22/11/1917	23/11/1917
War Diary	Dessart Wood	24/11/1917	27/11/1917
War Diary	Trescault	28/11/1917	28/11/1917
War Diary	Flesquieres	29/11/1917	30/11/1917
Heading	War Diary Of The 2/5th Battn The Lincolnshire Regiment From 1/12/17 To 31/12/17		
War Diary	Flesquieres	01/12/1917	02/12/1917
War Diary	Bourlon Wood	03/12/1917	04/12/1917
War Diary	Flesquieres	05/12/1917	09/12/1917
War Diary	Trescault	10/12/1917	10/12/1917
War Diary	Lechelle	11/12/1917	13/12/1917
War Diary	Trescault	13/12/1917	13/12/1917
War Diary	Havrincourt	14/12/1917	17/12/1917
War Diary	Flesquieres	17/12/1917	23/12/1917
War Diary	Rocquiny	24/12/1917	25/12/1917
War Diary	Ambrines	26/12/1917	31/12/1917
Heading	War Diary Of 2/5th Bn Lincolnshire Regiment From 1/1/18 To 31/1/18		
War Diary	Ambrines	01/01/1918	31/01/1918
Heading	War Diary Of The 2/5th Bn The Lincolnshire Regiment From 1/2/18 To 28/2/18		
War Diary	Ambrines I.4. (Sheet)	01/02/1918	09/02/1918
War Diary	Gouy-En Artois	09/02/1918	09/02/1918
War Diary	Blaireville	10/02/1918	10/02/1918
War Diary	Mory (8.2.sh 570)	11/02/1918	11/02/1918
War Diary	Bullecourt (U.27b.Sh.516 SW)	12/02/1918	24/02/1918
War Diary	Mory	25/02/1918	28/02/1918
Operation(al) Order(s)	2/5 Lincolnshire Regt Operation Order No. 56	08/02/1918	08/02/1918
Operation(al) Order(s)	2/5 Lincolnshire Regt Operation Order No. 57	09/02/1918	09/02/1918
Operation(al) Order(s)	2/5 Lincolnshire Regt Operation Order No. 58	10/02/1918	10/02/1918
Operation(al) Order(s)	2/5 Lincolnshire Regt Operation Order No. 59	12/02/1918	12/02/1918
Operation(al) Order(s)	Operation Order No 60	17/02/1918	17/02/1918
Operation(al) Order(s)	Operation Order No. 61	22/02/1918	22/02/1918
Miscellaneous	Warning Order	27/02/1918	27/02/1918
Heading	War Diary Of 2/5th Battalion The Lincolnshire Regiment March 1918		
Heading	War Diary Of The 2/5th Bn The Lincolnshire Regt From 1/3/18 To 31/3/18		
War Diary	Ecoust St. Mein C2 (57 NW)	01/03/1918	02/03/1918
War Diary	Bullecourt (U27 516 SW)	02/03/1918	14/03/1918
War Diary	Ecoust St. Mein C2 (57 NW)	15/03/1918	26/03/1918
War Diary	Sus St Leger	27/03/1918	29/03/1918
War Diary	Houdain	30/03/1918	31/03/1918
Miscellaneous	2/5th Bn The Lincolnshire Ref	21/03/1918	21/03/1918
Map	Map		
Map	France		
Heading	2/5th Battalion Lincolnshire Regiment April 1918		
Heading	War Diary Of The 2/5th Battalion The Lincolnshire Rgt From 1/4/18 To 30/4/18		
War Diary	Houdain	01/04/1918	01/04/1918
War Diary	Watou	01/04/1918	04/04/1918
War Diary	Zonnebeke	04/04/1918	10/04/1918
War Diary	St Jean	10/04/1918	12/04/1918
War Diary	Brandhoek	13/04/1918	13/04/1918
War Diary	Mont Des Cats	14/04/1918	14/04/1918

War Diary	Locre	14/04/1918	14/04/1918
War Diary	Bailleul	14/04/1918	16/04/1918
War Diary	Locre	17/04/1918	19/04/1918
War Diary	Reninghelst	20/04/1918	20/04/1918
War Diary	Brandhoek	21/04/1918	21/04/1918
War Diary	Houtkerque	21/04/1918	26/04/1918
War Diary	St Jan-Ter-Biezen	27/04/1918	27/04/1918
War Diary	Reninghelst	28/04/1918	30/04/1918
Operation(al) Order(s)	2/5 Lincoln Regt Order No 70	09/04/1918	09/04/1918
Miscellaneous	On Account Of The Part Taken By The 2/5th BN Lincolnshire Rgt In Operation Bailleul	15/04/1918	15/04/1918
Operation(al) Order(s)	2/5 Lincoln Regt Operation Order No. 69		
Operation(al) Order(s)	2/5 Lincoln Regt Operation Order No 68	31/03/1918	31/03/1918
Heading	War Diary Of The 2/5th Bn Lincoln Regt. For The Month Of May 1918		
Heading	War Diary Of The 2/5th Bn Lincolnshire Rgt From 1/5/18 To 31/5/18		
War Diary	Reninghelst	01/05/1918	05/05/1918
War Diary	Houtkerque	06/05/1918	06/05/1918
War Diary	St Momelin	06/05/1918	09/05/1918
War Diary	Mametz	10/05/1918	10/05/1918
War Diary	Pressy Les Pernes	11/05/1918	14/05/1918
War Diary	Estree Cauchie	15/05/1918	28/05/1918
War Diary	Allery	29/05/1918	31/05/1918
Heading	War Diary Of The 2/5th Bn The Lincolnshire Regiment From 1/6/18 To 30/6/18		
War Diary	Allery	01/06/1918	11/06/1918
War Diary	Monchaux	12/06/1918	12/06/1918
War Diary	Ch De La Haie	15/06/1918	15/06/1918
War Diary	Molliens An Bois	21/06/1918	21/06/1918
War Diary	Berteaucourt	27/06/1918	27/06/1918
War Diary	Monfliers	28/06/1918	30/06/1918
Operation(al) Order(s)	2/5 Lincolnshire Regt Operation Order No 127	12/06/1918	12/06/1918
Operation(al) Order(s)	2/5 Lincoln Regt Operation Order No 129	14/06/1918	14/06/1918
Heading	War Diary Of The 2/5th Bn The Lincolnshire Regt From 1/7/18 To 31/7/18		
War Diary	Monfliers	01/07/1918	01/07/1918
War Diary	Ribeaucourt	03/07/1918	03/07/1918
War Diary	Le Souich	04/07/1918	21/07/1918
War Diary	Candas	21/07/1918	22/07/1918
War Diary	Abancourt	23/07/1918	31/07/1918

59TH DIVISION
177TH INFY BDE

2-5TH BN LINCOLN REGT
FEB 1917 — JULY 1918

AND
1916 JAN & FEB

DISBANDED JULY 18

WO95/3023/5
2/5 Battalion Lincolnshire Regiment

Confidential

War Diary
of
2/5 Lincolnshire Regt.

From Jany 1st 1916 to Jany 31st 1916

H. Sumnutt Walker Colonel
Comdg 2/5th Lincolnshire Regt.

2/5-13 TH THE LINCOLNSHIRE REGT

Army Form C. 2118.

WAR DIARY
or
INTELLIGENCE SUMMARY.
(Erase heading not required.)

Instructions regarding War Diaries and Intelligence Summaries are contained in F.S. Regs., Part II. and the Staff Manual respectively. Title pages will be prepared in manuscript.

HEADQUARTERS 177th INFANTRY BRIGADE
No. S/151
3 – FEB. 1916

Hour, Date, Place	Summary of Events and Information	Remarks and references to Appendices
1-1-16 Harpenden	Strength of Battalion. 28 Officers (1 attached) 536 other ranks (260 trained) 1st Line Transport complete with exception of pack Saddlery. Machine guns have not yet been issued.	JCS
10-1-16 do	Capt F.P. Sturm R.A.M.C attached as Medical Officer	JCS
24-1-16 do	2/Lts J.B. Coulson and F.R. Coulson transferred to 3/5 Lincoln Regt. under provisions of M.O.L. 9/9 Infantry/2. (T.F.3)	JCS
27-1-16 do	Major E. Sleight, attached from 1/5 Lincoln Regt. posted to 25th Provisional Batt.	JCS
29-1-16 do	59 Derby recruits taken in strength. These men called up under Lord Derby's Scheme being Army Reserve Class B	JCS
31-1-16 do	44 Derby recruits taken in strength.	JCS

Smithson Colonel
Cmdg 2/5/5 Lincolnshire Regt

Confidential

War Diary
of
2/5 Lincolnshire Regt.

from 31/1/16 to 22/2/1916.

.... Colonel
Commdg. 2/5th Battn. Lincoln Regt.

Army Form C. 2118.

WAR DIARY or INTELLIGENCE SUMMARY.
(Erase heading not required.)

Instructions regarding War Diaries and Intelligence Summaries are contained in F.S. Regs., Part II. and the Staff Manual respectively. Title pages will be prepared in manuscript.

ORDERLY ROOM
29 FEB 1916
2/5th BN. LINCOLN REGT.

Place	Date	Hour	Summary of Events and Information	Remarks and references to Appendices
Harpenden	31/1/16	-	Zeppelin Raid on Midland Counties. Alarm received here 10.15 pm. 31/1/16 but no air craft appeared.	pay
	1/2/16		47 recruits taken on strength.	gcu
do.	3/2/16		33 recruits taken on strength.	gcu
do.	7/2/16		27 do do do	gcu
do.	10/2/16		25 do do do	gcu
do.	11/2/16		57 do do do	gcu
do.	12/2/16		30 do do do	gcu
do.	14/2/16		12 do do do. The total complement of Derby recruits having been received and Strength of battalion less men awaiting discharge now 550 other ranks	gcu
do.	17/2/16		CAPT. H.G. MADDISON promoted MAJOR and took over duties of 2nd in command from this date.	gcu
do.	22/2/16		3rd Army Letter 6590/A.Q. states that War Establishments Part VIII now applies to this unit. Mobilization Store Table A.7. 9.1095-110 also applies from this date.	gcu

Shuttleworth Colonel
Comg 2/5 Lincolnshire Regt.

WO95/3023/3/4

2/5 Battalion Lincolnshire Regiment

2/5 BN LINCOLNSHIRE REGT 17/1/59 SECRET

Army Form C. 2118.

WAR DIARY
INTELLIGENCE SUMMARY
(Erase heading not required.)

February 1917 Vol 1

Instructions regarding War Diaries and Intelligence Summaries are contained in F.S. Regs., Part II. and the Staff Manual respectively. Title Pages will be prepared in manuscript.

Place	Date	Hour	Summary of Events and Information	Remarks and references to Appendices
FOVANT	23/2/17	11.40	A Coy plus one platoon of B Coy entrained at DINTON for SOUTHAMPTON.	
SOUTHAMPTON	"	12.50	Remainder of Battalion entrained for SOUTHAMPTON. 105 other ranks remained in ENGLAND.	
		19.00	Embarked on S.S. Connaught for LE HAVRE. Following officers proceeded with Battalion. Lieut Colonel H.B. Roffey, Major G.M. Madeley, Capt. A.H. Worrall, Capt & Adjutant J.C. Urquhart, Captains T. Bryant, M. Fitzpatrick, C.N. Newsum, F.S. Letten, G.L. Hill, Lieutenants J.S. Simons, G. Goodman, J.W. Walker, E.G. Butler, 2nd Lieutenants F.B. Letts, R.H. Turner, W.L. Rudall, M.T. Chambers, H.W.C. Chambers, (3rd Essex Rgt.) C.A.L. Wiles (3rd Lincolns), B.V.S. Poyser, Lieut & Q.M. R.H. Lewis, Capt. F.P. Sturm. R.A.M.C.	
LE HAVRE	24.2.17	8.0	Disembarked at LE HAVRE and proceeded to No. 5 Rest Camp. No. in frame 29 officers 907 O.R.	
		12.30	A Coy plus one platoon of B Coy entrained at Point 3. GARE des MARCHANDISES.	
		19.30	Remainder of Battalion entrained at Point 1. Gare des Marchandises.	
LE SALEUX	25.2.17	14.30	A Coy plus 1 platoon of B Coy detrained at LE SALEUX and proceeded to BACOUEL by march route and went into billets.	
		16.30	Remainder of battalion detrained at LE SALEUX and proceeded to BACOUEL by march route and went into billets, arriving 18.15.	
BACOUEL		18.15	Companies billeted in order A.B.C.D. at le Mairie and School.	
do.	26.2.17		Inspection of Kit, transport equipment.	
do.	27.2.17	10.0	Battalion proceeds by March Route to FOUENCAMPS and went into billets. Companies billeted along main road in order A.B.C.D. running N to S. Following issues were made - one additional blanket per man (each mess mask). 2) one bread cover per rifle and Lewis gun.	see appendix
FOUENCAMPS		15.30	Companies billeted along main road in order A.B.C.D. running N to S.	

2449 Wt. W14957/M90 750,000 1/16 J.B.C. & A. Forms/C.2118/12.

Army Form C. 2118.

WAR DIARY
INTELLIGENCE SUMMARY
(Erase heading not required.)

Place	Date	Hour	Summary of Events and Information	Remarks and references to Appendices
FOUENCAMPS	28.2.17	9.0	Battalion proceeded by march route to BAYONVILLERS arriving 15.15. Billeted in RUE de LAMOTTE, N. end of village.	See Appendix II. Jan

K.R.M. Murphy Lt. Colonel
Cmdg. 2/5 Lincolnshire Regt.

Appendix I

2/5 LINCOLN. REGT. Order No. 1.

Ref. 3rd Army Area. Admn. Map.　　　　　　　　26.2.17.

Intention 1. The Bn. — order of march as per margin — will route march to FOUENCAMPS on 27.2.17.

H.Q.
A.B.C.D.Coys.

Transport. 2. The transport will proceed via the route detailed to the Transport Officer. Officers Mess Cart and Maltese Cart will accompany the Bn.

Baggage. 3. All officers Kits and Officers Mess Boxes will be sent to Bn H.Q. at 8.30. a.m. Blankets will be tied in Bundles of 10, labelled by companies and stacked at Coy H.Q. Each coy will leave 1 NCO & 6 men to load these on the Motor lorries. When loaded, these parties will report to Capt. C.N. Newsum at Bn H.Q. Capt. Newsum will report to H.Q. at 6.30 p.m. tonight for orders.

Starting Pt. 4. Head of column will be at the road junction at the Convent Gate at 10. a.m.

Reports. 5. Reports to head of main body.

　　　　　　　　　　　　　　J.C.Ingham. Capt. & Adjt.

Copies. No.1 retained　　　Bn.Route. BACOUEL – DURY –
Nos. 2-5. ABCD Coys.　　　　　　ST. FUSCIEN – BOVES
No. 6. Q.M.　　　　　　　　　　– FOUEN CAMPS.
No. 7 Transport Officer.　　Transport Route. BACOUEL – AMIENS
Issued at. 18.00　　　　　ST. ACHIEL – LONGUEAU – ST. NICOLAS
　　26.2.17　　　　　　　– FOUEN CAMPS.　J.C.Ingham
　　　　　　　　　　　　　　　　　　　　Capt. & Adjt.

APPENDIX II.

2/5 Lincoln Regt. Order No 2
Ref. 30dd?? Area Admin. Map.   27-2-17

Intention   1. The Bn will route march to GRAYONVILLE R.S.
H.Q.   Order of march as per margin on 28-2-17
B.C.D.A Coys
Transport

Baggage   2. H.Q. officers' Kits will be carried on Baggage
               wagons of train.
               H.Q. & Coy blankets will be rolled, labelled and
               packed on Mechanical Transport at 8 a.m.
               together with Company Officers' Kits.

Starting Point 3. Headquarters will pass under the
                  Bridge at N end of village at 9 a.m.

Reports   4. Reports to head of main body.

                                           J C M S ????
Copies.   Capt & Adjt
Not retained   2/5 Lincoln Regt.
1 2 3 4 5 A B C D Coys
6   Transport Officer
7   Quartermaster
8   M.O.
9   Lt Goodman

Issued at 18.30   27.2.17.

Army Form C. 2118.

CONFIDENTIAL

WAR DIARY MARCH 1917.
or
INTELLIGENCE SUMMARY
(Erase heading not required.)

Instructions regarding War Diaries and Intelligence Summaries are contained in F.S. Regs., Part II. and the Staff Manual respectively. Title Pages will be prepared in manuscript.

2/5th Lincoln Regt.

All map references except where otherwise stated are to sheet 62.C. S.W. FRANCE

Place	Date	Hour	Summary of Events and Information	Remarks and references to Appendices
BAYONVILLERS	1.3.17		Strength of Battalion 29 officers, 909 O.R. 3 men admitted to hospital sick. Day devoted to inspections of Kit and internal economy, drill and bayonet fighting.	
BAYONVILLERS	2.3.17.		All ranks passed into Smoke Box Respirator. The P.H. helmet has now been withdrawn. 7 men admitted to hospital sick. Training continued. Drill, Bayonet fighting, Lewis gun classes.	
– do –	3.3.17.		Training continued. B.O. Adjutant, Bombing and Intelligence Officers proceed to front line trenches preparatory to relief of front line units by this battalion. Attached to 5th B. Durham Light Infantry whom the battalion will relieve in the front line trenches.	See appendix III
– do –	4.3.17		Routine work continued. The Battalion Bombing Officer, Lieut G. GOODMAN was wounded in the right arm at 11.50 p.m. while in front line trench at N.34.b.7.0. One platoon per company sent up into the front line preparatory to relief. Ten instructors were attached to companies 2/Lt 5th D.L.I.	See appendix III
– do –	5.3.17		Training continued - Lewis gun classes, Gas helmet drill. Bayonet fighting.	
– do –	6.3.17	7.45 am	Battalion route marched from BAYONVILLERS to TRIANGLE COPSE (map reference M.17.C.8.7.) and were accommodated in dugouts & shelters. C Coy at M.17.C.7.7. B Coy at M.10 d.9.5.	See appendix IV

WAR DIARY
or
INTELLIGENCE SUMMARY

(Erase heading not required.)

Army Form C. 2118.

Instructions regarding War Diaries and Intelligence Summaries are contained in F. S. Regs., Part II. and the Staff Manual respectively. Title Pages will be prepared in manuscript.

Place	Date	Hour	Summary of Events and Information	Remarks and references to Appendices
TRIANGLE COPSE.	7.3.17	5.30. p.m.	Relief of 5th Bn. Durham Light Infantry on front line trenches commenced owing to the impassable state of the communication trenches - knee deep in mud - the relief was carried out over the top and was accomplished without casualties, and was completed without hitch.	see Appendix #I Jay.
Trenches Front Line.	7.3.17.	11.15p.m.	Relief reports complete. The line now held by the Battalion is the left Sub Sector of the Sector allotted to the 177th Infantry Brigade and runs between the limits N.25.d.9.4 and N.34.d.5.5. The scheme of defence was as in appendix VI and was carried on similar instructions of G.O.C. 177th Infantry Brigade. Bending the name of junta orders. The front line appeared to be too strongly held the Battalion was in touch on the left flank with troops of the 1st Division - Trench Mortars and on the right flank with the 94th Bn. Lincolnshire Regt. The trenches are in a very bad condition and communication trenches are in most cases impassable.	Jay
FRONT LINE TRENCHES.	8.3.17		Working parties at work on clearing of communication trenches. Some progress was made but scoops are really necessary to remove mud. 5 men wounded with grenade fire. This appears to be the chief missile in this area. The lines were bombarded with grenades during most of the day. A few rounds of shrapnel were also sent over. On the whole the enemy is very quiet and this line appears	

Army Form C. 2118.

Instructions regarding War Diaries and Intelligence Summaries are contained in F. S. Regs., Part II. and the Staff Manual respectively. Title Pages will be prepared in manuscript.

WAR DIARY
or
INTELLIGENCE SUMMARY
(Erase heading not required.)

Place	Date	Hour	Summary of Events and Information	Remarks and references to Appendices
FRONT LINE TRENCHES	8.3.17		to be very thinly held. Our dispositions are 360 men in front lines, 180 in Support and 180 in reserve, 3 men wounded by Grenades.	
-do-	9.3.17		Situation still quiet. Many hits have been observed in the enemy's Support trenches and behind his lines. Very little firing. Our patrols have been inactive owing to bright moonlight. Rifle company relief was carried out. Present dispositions C & D Company in front line. B in support. A in reserve.	Given
-do-	10.3.17		Situation still quiet. The line was shelled intermittently during the day by fish tail bombs. Condition of trenches much better owing to frost.	
-do-	10.3.17	12:0 mid.	An officer patrol under 2/Lieut. R.H. TURNER went out at 12 midnight did not return.	
-do-	11.3.17		Have had rest in and trenches are rapidly becoming impassable. Cleaning work is being continued but there is no easy communication from front to rear via communication trenches.	
-do-	-do-	8.35pm	The patrol reported as missing on 10.3.17 returned having lain out in a shell hole all day, about 30 yards from German wire. They report work proceeding in enemy trenches and gave information on enemy's wire - thick & deep.	
-do-	-do-	9.0pm	B. Coy relieved front line posts of D Coy as the men of latter company were exhausted. Mud very bad in front line trenches.	Given

Army Form C. 2118.

WAR DIARY
or
INTELLIGENCE SUMMARY
(Erase heading not required.)

Instructions regarding War Diaries and Intelligence Summaries are contained in F. S. Regs., Part II. and the Staff Manual respectively. Title Pages will be prepared in manuscript.

Place	Date	Hour	Summary of Events and Information	Remarks and references to Appendices
FRONT LINE TRENCHES.	12.3.17	5.0 a.m.	Under the previous arrangements the Battalion should have been relieved on the night of 11th–12th but this was delayed. The front line trench is in a very bad condition and the men are very exhausted after 3 days. It has been necessary to dig men out of the mud.	
		7.30 a.m.	Captain A. H. WORRALL wounded – rifle bullet through left elbow. Captain C. N. NEWSUM (second in command of 'C' Coy in front line. Situation quiet all day. A few bursts of rapid fire were sent over. Casualties 1 man killed, 1 man wounded.	
		7.30 p.m.	Two officers in German reserve lines. Relief by 9/5 B. Leicestershire Regt. commenced. All parts retired on the top.	See Appendix VII
		11.45 p.m.	Relief completed. Companies moved independently to TRIANGLE WOOD to dug-outs. This is at 17.17. C.F.7. The position of the Battalion in reserve.	
TRIANGLE WOOD.	13.3.17		Day devoted to bathing and interior economy. Particular attention is paid to bathing of feet with potash soap and dusting with talc powder. This is to prevent trench feet. No of cases in this unit since 7.3.17 is 10. 7 of which has not been able to have the prophylactic treatment. Several small items of equipment have been lost in the mud. Steps have been taken to ensure a new supply is forthcoming.	
– do –	14.3.17		Training continued. Box respirators tested in lachrymatory Gas. (200 Strong) were found satisfactory.	

Army Form C. 2118.

WAR DIARY
or
INTELLIGENCE SUMMARY
(Erase heading not required.)

Instructions regarding War Diaries and Intelligence Summaries are contained in F.S. Regs., Part II. and the Staff Manual respectively. Title Pages will be prepared in manuscript.

Place	Date	Hour	Summary of Events and Information	Remarks and references to Appendices
TRIANGLE WOOD.	14.3.17		On Reserve and communication trenches.	
— do —	15.3.17		Training continued. Working parties found as for 14.3.17. Lieut. B.V.S. POYSER wounded by shrapnel while in charge of a working party at Trench LEDUC. Bathing for men at Brigade Baths at FAY. Situation in line still quiet.	
	10.50.		Major H.G. MADELEY admitted to hospital with laryngitis. The following officers are back in hospital Capt F.S. LETTEN, LIEUT. W.H.N. HEWER. 2/Lieuts G.J. PEARSON, F.D. EMERY, M.T. CHAMBERS.	
— do —	16.3.17		Training continued. Bathing continued. Clean clothing has been issued to all NCOs and men from Divisional Laundry. Capt F.P. STURM. R.A.M.C. having been admitted to hospital sick, Capt. W.P. TINDALE ATKINSON R.A.M.C.T took over duties of Medical Officer to the battalion. Situation very quiet. It is believed that the enemy have withdrawn EAST of the R. SOMME. All working parties cancelled.	
— do —	17.3.17 10.30am.		Orders received to be in readiness to move forward as enemy had withdrawn from this trenches. Rations for the 18.3.17 were brought up and held in readiness to move, and arrangements made for bringing up rations on horses in case the battalion moved forward. The roads are impassable for limbers wagons.	See Appendix VIII.

Army Form C. 2118.

WAR DIARY
or
INTELLIGENCE SUMMARY.
(Erase heading not required.)

Instructions regarding War Diaries and Intelligence Summaries are contained in F.S. Regs., Part II. and the Staff Manual respectively. Title pages will be prepared in manuscript. Map reference.

Place	Hour, Date	Summary of Events and Information	Remarks and references to Appendices
		FRANCE. 62.C.S.W.	
TRIANGLE WOOD.	18.3.17 3.45 pm	A.C and D Companies moved into support trenches in Area N.28 c and d; Bn. H.Q at P.C. NANCY N.28 d.2.4. Battalion is now Brigade Support Battalion and is in touch with the 2/4th and 2/5th LEICESTER Rgt at HORGNY and ANTIC WOOD AREA. Distribution. A. Coy. N.34 & 3.6. C Coy. N.28.c 8.4. D. Coy. N. 2 F d. 6.5.	see APPENDIX VIII JCW
TRENCHES as for 18.3.17	19.3.17.	Day and night working parties found for repair of ESTREES - VILLERS CARBONNEL road which is in bad condition. Situation unchanged and very quiet.	JCW
- do -	20.3.17	Repair of ESTREES - VILLERS CARBONNEL road continued. The enemy appears to have retreated some considerable distance E. of the R. SOMME. Many fires were seen in the E beyond the river	JCW
- do -	21.3.17 1.0 pm.	Support trenches evacuated and see trench and area above were handed over to 5th Sherwood Foresters, 178th Infty. Bde. Battalion proceeded to FOUCAUCOURT and into rest billets. H.Q. M.33 a. 2.7.	JCW

Army Form C. 2118.

WAR DIARY
or
INTELLIGENCE SUMMARY.
(Erase heading not required.)

Instructions regarding War Diaries and Intelligence Summaries are contained in F.S. Regs., Part II and the Staff Manual respectively. Title pages will be prepared in manuscript.

Hour, Date, Place		Summary of Events and Information	Remarks and references to Appendices
FOUCAUCOURT.	22.3.17	Interior Economy. Cleaning, bathing, kit rifle and equipment inspections.	Jw
— do —	23.3.17	As for 22.3.17	Jw
— do —	24.3.17	Reorganization of Platoons as laid down in O.B/1919. Each platoon now has 1 Section riflemen, 1 Section rifle grenadiers, 1 Section bombers, 1 Section Lewis Gunners. Batting continued.	Jw
— do —	25.3.17 1.0 p.m.	Bn. proceeded by march route to ETERPIGNY.	see Appendix X
ETERPIGNY	25.3.17 3.45 p.m.	Distribution A. Coy. 0.20.a.8.3. B. Coy. 0.25.6.88 C. Coy. 0.19.6.5.5 D. Coy. 0.20.a.3.10. H.Q. 0.20.c.4.4. Brigade H.Q. PRIORY at ETERPIGNY.	Jw
ETERPIGNY.	26.3.17	Bn. proceeded by march route to BEAUMETZ and took up outpost line.	See Appendix XI
BEAUMETZ	26.3.17	Dispositions. Outpost line. Ref. Sheet 62c S.E. FRANCE. Outposts. No.1 Coy. (A) P.18.a.4.6. passing E. of BEAUMETZ 2 cross roads P.12.6.3.3. inclusive. No.2 Coy. from left of No.1 to word K.31.c and K.31.d (southern portion) inclusive Q.1.6.8.9.) Two Companies in reserve at ELAM COPSE (P.5.d.3.1.)	

Army Form C. 2118.

WAR DIARY
or
INTELLIGENCE SUMMARY.
(Erase heading not required.)

Instructions regarding War Diaries and Intelligence Summaries are contained in F.S. Regs., Part II and the Staff Manual respectively. Title pages will be prepared in manuscript.

Map references to FRANCE SHEET. 62 c.

Hour, Date, Place		Summary of Events and Information	Remarks and references to Appendices
BEAUMETZ.	26.3.17	Dispositions (cont'd). Bn. H.Q. at P.11 & 10.7. Touch established with 2/7th SHERWOOD FORESTERS at BOUVINCOURT, with 18th BENGAL LANCERS at HANCOURT and with 2/4th LINCOLN Rgt at BOUCLY, and at Q.1.b.9.10.	
BEAUMETZ.	July 26. 27 3.17. 6.0 pm	Bn. proceeded by march route to NOBESCOURT FARM. (K.32.b.9.1.) and took up an outpost line. Dispositions Outpost line held by 1 company from Q.3.b.9.5 along BERNES - HAMELET ROAD to K.27.c.6.9. 3 companies and H.Q. at NOBESCOURT FARM.	Jw.
NOBESCOURT FARM.	27.3.17 8.0pm.	The farm was shelled intermittently from 8 lights field gun. Outpost patrols have not come into contact with enemy. Outpost line is in touch with 2/4th LINCOLN Rgt on left at K.27.c and with 2/7th SHERWOOD FORESTERS at BERNES.	Jw.
— do —	28.3.17 9.0 am.	Four points were selected at K.33.d.4.4. K.33.c.9.7. K.33.a.9.7 and K.27.c.3.2. at which Cruciform Posts are to be dug as a nucleus of Divisional Main Line of Resistance. Selected by III Corps & Div. H.Q. G.S.O's.	
	2.0 pm.		
	8.0 pm.	Work commenced on cruciform posts and wiring round and between them.	Jw.

Army Form C. 2118.

WAR DIARY
or
INTELLIGENCE SUMMARY.
(Erase heading not required.)

Instructions regarding War Diaries and Intelligence Summaries are contained in F.S. Regs., Part II and the Staff Manual respectively. Title pages will be prepared in manuscript.

Hour, Date, Place	Summary of Events and Information	Remarks and references to Appendices
NOBESCOURT FARM 29.3.17. 8.0 pm	Work continued on main line of resistance. Posts dispersed wire strengthened and extended. Enemy very quiet.	
– do – 30.3.17.	Work continued - support line in main line of Resistance commenced by digging 100 yards of wire in rear of each outpost post.	
– do – 31.3.17.	Work continued on Outpost posts wire and support line. Enemy very quiet. Outpost patrol reports meeting enemy patrol in vicinity of K.28.a.9.1. Otherwise enemy not seen. A few shells were thrown into the farm during the day. 10.p.m. Capropalm Adj. 4.8 Lewis gunners and 24 Scouts Snipers of this unit under Lieut. T.S. SIMONS took part in an attack on HESBECOURT by 2/5 LEICESTER RGT. Casualties 4 Other Ranks wounded.	

W.M.M.M.T.
Lieut. Colonel
Cmdg 2/5 Lincolnshire Rgt

War Diary

SECRET.

Copy No: 3

177th INFANTRY BRIGADE OPERATION ORDER NO: 1.

4th March, 1917.

1. 177th Inf.Brigade will relieve 150th Inf.Brigade in accordance with attached Table.

2. Rendezvous for guides and all other details of relief to be arranged between Units concerned.

3. O.C., Units will take over all maps, photographs and schemes from Unit they relieve.

4. A report will be sent to Brigade Major, 177th Inf.Brigade at P.C.BULOW, when each relief is completed.

5. Brigadier General Commanding 177th Inf. Brigade will assume command of Left Divisional Sub-sector at 10 A.M., 9th March.

6. Brigade H.Qrs. will close at BAYONVILLERS at 9 A.M. 9th March and open at same hour at P.C. BULOW.

Acknowledge.

Issued at 4 P.M.

By D. R. L. S.

Major,
Brigade Major,
177th Infantry Brigade.

Copy No: 1. Filed.
2. 4th Lincs.
3. 5th Lincs.
4. 4th Leicesters.
5. 5th Leicesters.
6. Lt-Col.JOHNSON.
7. Lt-Col.ROFFEY.
8. Lt-Col.WALLIS.
9. 177th M.G.Coy.
10. Capt.SHEFFIELD.
11. 177th T.M.Bty.
12. Capt.HOWARD.
13. 59th Division.
14. 59th Division.
15. 3rd Inf.Brigade.
16. 151st Inf.Brigade.
17. 150th Inf.Brigade.
18. Bde.Transport Officer.
19. Bde.Signalling Officer.
20. War Diary.
21. Staff Captain.
22. Spare.
23. "
24. Office.

MARCH TABLE ISSUED WITH 177TH INFANTRY BRIGADE OPERATION ORDER NO.1. 4.3.17.   S E C R E T.

Date	UNIT	FROM	TO	TO RELIEVE	HOUR OF START	ROUTE	REMARKS.
March 5th	4th Lincolns	BAYONVILLERS	FOUCAUCOURT		9 a.m.	Main AMIENS Rd.	
6th	5th Lincolns	BAYONVILLERS	BOIS TRIANGULAIRE	4th East Yorks.	9 a.m.	Main AMIENS-ESTRÉES Road.	
6th/7th	4th Lincolns	FOUCAUCOURT	Right front line	5th Yorks.Rgt.			
7th	4th Leicesters	BAYONVILLERS	FOUCAUCOURT	5th Yorks.Rgt.	12.30 p.m.	Main AMIENS Rd.	
7th/8th	5th Lincolns	BOIS TRIANGULAIRE	Left front line	5th Durham L.I.			
8th	5th Leicesters	Camp 59 BAYONVILLERS	BOIS TRIANGULAIRE	5th Durham L.I.	12.30 p.m.	Main AMIENS-ESTRÉES Rd.	Take blankets.
8th/9th	4th Leicesters	FOUCAUCOURT	BELLOY	4th Yorks.Rgt.			
6th	177 M.G.Coy.	BAYONVILLERS	CHUIGNES CAMP		To be arranged by O.C.	Main AMIENS Road.	
7th	Half 177th M.G.Coy.	CHUIGNES	Half 150th M.G.Coy. Line				
8th	Half 177th M.G.Coy.	CHUIGNES	Half 150th M.G.Coy. Line				

(2).

MARCH TABLE (2)

DATE	UNIT	FROM	TO	TO RELIEVE	HOUR OF START	ROUTE
March 4th	177th Light T.M. Bty.	BAYONVILLERS	CIMIFIERE CAMP		To be arranged by O.C.	Main AMIENS Road.
5th/6th	Half 177th T.M. Bty.	CIMIFIERE CAMP	Line	Half 119th T.M.Bty.		
6th/7th	Half 177th T.M.Bty.	CIMIFIERE CAMP.	Line	Half 119th T.M.Bty.		
5th	SIGNAL SECTION (Sergt.Slade - 4 Operators) (1 driver with cart and) (all instruments.)		March to FOUCAUCOURT with 4th Lincolns on morning of 6th. Will receive orders from O.C.,signal section re further move forward.			
7th	SIGNAL SECTION (remainder)		March to FOUCAUCOURT with 4th Leicesters. On 7th proceed to Brigade headquarters,150th Infantry brigade.			

Intervals of 100 yards to be kept between companies and every 12 vehicles.

War Diary
Appendix IV

SECRET

Copy No. 4

AMENDMENT TO 177TH INFANTRY BRIGADE OPERATION
ORDER No.1. Dated 4. 3. 17.

6th March 1917.

Para 6.:- Brigade headquarters will close
at BAYONVILLERS at 9.0 A.M. 6th March
and open at same hour at P.C.BULOW.

Major,
Brigade Major,
177th Infantry Brigade.

Distribution as for Operation Order No.1.

APPENDIX VII

S E C R E T.

COPY NO 4

177th INFANTRY BRIGADE OPERATION ORDER NO 3.

Ref Sheet 62 c S.W.   10.3.17.

1. Following inter-battalion reliefs will take place on nights 11/12 and 12/13 March.

2. 4th Leicester Regt will relieve 4th Lincoln Regt in right sub-sector on night 11/12 March. On relief 4th Lincoln Regt will go into support at BELLOY.

3. 5th Leicester Regt will relieve 5th Lincoln Regt in left sub-sector on night 12/13 March on relief 5th Lincoln Regt will go into reserve at BOIS - TRIANGULAIRE.

4. All other details of relief will be made direct between O.C. battalions.

5. All photographs, maps, schemes, trench stores etc will be handed over.

6. Outgoing Battalions will be responsible for patrolling up to time of relief is complete and will hand over information received by these patrols to relieving unit who will be responsible for all reports etc after taking over.

7. Completion of relief to be notified in code to Brigade Headquarters.

8. Acknowledge.

Major.
Brigade Major.
177th Infantry Brigade.

Copy No. 1. Filed.   No 8. 3rd Inf Brigade.
"   "   2. H.Q. 59th Division.   " 9. 177th Machine Gun Co.
"   "   3. 4th Lincoln Regt.   " 10. 177th Trench Mtr Bty.
"   "   4. 5th Lincoln Regt.   " 11. Staff Captain.
"   "   5. 4th Leicester Regt.   " 12. Left sub group 50th D.A.
"   "   6. 5th Leicester Regt.   " 13. War diary.
"   "   7. H.Q. 176th Inf Bde.   " 14. War diary.

Appendix XIV

Operation Order   No. 12
2/5th Bn Lincolnshire Regt.   19.4.17
Ref. Sheet 62c NE & SE.

1. The Bn. will be relieved in the trenches tonight 19.4.17 by the 2/6th Bn. Sherwood Foresters.

2. 'D' Coy will be relieved by 'A' Coy S.F.
   'B' " " " " 'B' " S.F.
   'C' " " " " 'C' " S.F.
   'D' " S.F. will go into reserve at Bn. H.Q.

3. 'D' 'B' and 'C' Coys will each send 4 guides (1 per platoon) to Bn H.Q. at 3.0 p.m. this afternoon. In case of 'D' and 'B' Coys these guides must know the positions of the posts.

4. Coys on relief will proceed to VRAIGNES into billets and will be met at the entrance to the village by guides to conduct to billets.

5. All trench stores will be handed over including tools, wire, stakes etc. All material and stores to be handed over must be collected into suitable heaps. Trench covers will be handed over. Lewis Gun panniers will be dumped at ration dump as Companies pass and will be loaded on to limber there.
   Receipts will be taken for all stores.

6. Relief complete will be reported to Bn. HQ.

                                    J Chnr...
                                    Capt & Adjt
                                    2/5th Lincoln Regt.

19.4.17

5. Copies of Receipt for trench Stores will be rendered to Bn. H.Q. by 9 a.m. 29/4/17
6. Fighting Kit will be worn with blanket and waterproof. Rations for tomorrow will be carried by the men.
7. Coy. boundries will send to H.Q. as soon as possible the Map references of their posts and Coy. H.Q.
8. Relief complete will be reported to Bn H.Q. Code word GOUDLE.

Copy No. 1 Retained
- 2.3.4.5 A.B.C.&D Coys
- 6 T.O.
- 7 Q. Mr.
- 8 H.Q. Coy
- 9 L.G. Officer
- 10 & 11 War Diary
- 12 R.S.M.

J Hersey
Capt & Adjt
2/5th Bn Lincoln Regt.

28.4.17

APPENDIX XV

2/5th Lincoln Regt.   Operation Order No 13
          Ref, Sheet. 62c & 62b.   28.4.17

1. The 2/5th Bn. Lincoln Regt. will relieve the 2/5th Bn. N. Stafford Regt. in the front line tonight.

2. 'A' Coy 2/5th Lincoln Regt will relieve 'A' Coy 2/5th N. Staff. Regt.
   'B'   "   "   "   "   "   'B'   "   "   "
   'C'   "   "   "   "   "   'C'   "   "   "
   'D'   "   "   "   "   "   'D'   "   "   "

3. Platoons will leave VRAIGNES at intervals of 200x. H.Q leave at 6.25 p.m. 'C' Coy's first platoon will leave at 6.30 p.m. Remaining Coys follow in order B. D. A
   Guides will meet Coys at L.26.c.2.2.
        'C' Coy   4 guides
        'B' "   2   do
         D   "   3   do
         A   "   3   do

4. Lewis Guns and panniers will be dumped at Bn H.Q. by the transport together with petrol tins, Coke, Braziers and other Coy stores. Medical stores will also be dumped here. Lieut Boardley will supervise the issue of Lewis Guns and stores.
Transport Officer will arrange for a water cart to be brought full to Bn. H.Q. This cart will be filled twice daily by water duty men. Transport Officer will arrange for horses to be sent out for this work

(1)

Army Form C. 2118.

WAR DIARY
or
INTELLIGENCE SUMMARY

(Erase heading not required.)

Vol 3

CONFIDENTIAL

WAR DIARY

of

2/5th Bn. The LINCOLNSHIRE REGT.

from

1st April 1917 to 30th April 1917.

W.M.W.
Lieut. Colonel
Cmdg. 2/5th Bn Lincolnshire Regt.

In the field
1.5.17

Army Form C. 2118.

FRANCE.

Map Reference. Sheet 62 c N E

WAR DIARY
or
INTELLIGENCE SUMMARY.
(Erase heading not required.)

Instructions regarding War Diaries and Intelligence Summaries are contained in F.S. Regs., Part II and the Staff Manual respectively. Title pages will be prepared in manuscript.

Place	Hour, Date	Summary of Events and Information	Remarks and references to Appendices
NOBESCOURT FARM.	1.4.17.	Work on Cruciform posts and Support line continued.	JCW JFM
- do -	2.4.17.	One OR wounded while working on crater at K.33.a.9.4.	JFM
		Work on cruciform posts and support line of Divisional main line continued. One dug out on the Battalion section and M/G emplacements constructed. Nine has been erected round posts and between them.	
- do -	3.4.17.	Work continued as for 2.4.17.	JCW JFM
- do -	4.4.17.	Battalion resting in preparation for attack on enemy's position at night.	JCW JFM
	12.0 m.n.	Orders for attack cancelled.	JFM
- do -	6.4.17	Orders received to move to TEMPLEUX.	
	4.10 pm	Bn. proceeded by March route to ROISEL when orders were received to halt and billet for the night. Their accommodation in ruins in S. portion of town. Enemy very quiet.	
ROISEL	6.4.17.	Battalion resting 24 hours in preparation for attack at night. attack	JCW JFM
- do -	12.30pm	postponed indefinitely until further orders.	JCW
	5.0 pm	Reconnaissances by Company Officers. Battalion resting	JCW JFM
- do -	7.4.17	As for 7.4.17.	JCW
- do -	8.4.17		JCW
- do -	9.4.17 5.0 pm	Battalion moved by march route to TEMPLEUX in readiness for attack. On arrival at TEMPLEUX information was received that the Germans had retired from the position to be attacked and that the 4th LINCOLN REGT were now taking	

WAR DIARY or INTELLIGENCE SUMMARY.

Army Form C. 2118.

(Erase heading not required.)

Instructions regarding War Diaries and Intelligence Summaries are contained in F.S. Regs., Part II and the Staff Manual respectively. Title pages will be prepared in manuscript.

References to Maps. France. Sheet 62 c. N.E.

Hour, Date, Place		Summary of Events and Information	Remarks and references to Appendices
TEMPLEUX.	9.4.17. 6.30pm.	Possession of the position. Fresh orders were received from Brigade H.Q. that the unit would take on the captured position and establish an outpost line from L.11.a.9.5 along EAST side of HARGICOURT to point L.4.b.6. which point to situate in the German trench and was to form been of bombing operations along German trench to MALAKOFF FARM. (F.30.c.) Owing to the German trench being commanded by the QUARRY in L.5.d. it was found impossible to hold point L.5.a.9.5. (The German trench was very 2 feet deep at the point, nor was it found possible to dig a cuneiform post at L.5.e.5.1. owing to heavy enemy fire. Posts were consequently established as follows L.11.a.4.7. L.4.d.7.3. L.5.c.2.8. L.4.b.6.5. L.4.b.3.6. This line was held by two companies with our supports at road passing through L.4.d.2.0 and sunken road in L.4.a. respectively. One company in Support in QUARRY in L.3.a., Bn. H.Q. and 1 company in reserve at L.3.b.1.0. Communication was established on left flank with 7th LEICESTER REGT. and on right flank with	
HARGICOURT.	11.0 pm.		
— do —	10.4.17. 12.0 noon.	Dispositions unchanged. Our line was constantly shelled during the night. Attempts to look down German trench to MALAKOFF FARM (F.30.c.) were frustrated by enemy M.G. fire from COLOGNE FARM and the Quarry in L.5.d.	

Army Form C. 2118.

WAR DIARY or INTELLIGENCE SUMMARY

(Erase heading not required.)

Instructions regarding War Diaries and Intelligence Summaries are contained in F.S. Regs., Part II. and the Staff Manual respectively. Title Pages will be prepared in manuscript.

References to France. Sheet 62c. S.E.

Place	Date	Hour	Summary of Events and Information	Remarks and references to Appendices
HARGICOURT	10.4.17	6.0pm	Information received that the 7th WORCESTERS on our left were advancing as far as the sunken Cross Roads in F.29.b. which was strongly held by the enemy. Orders were received at the same time to take every advantage of their advance and to push our post forward, and to bomb down the enemy trench from HARGICOURT to MALAKOFF FARM, and to capture the QUARRY in L.5.d. and COLOGNE FARM in route. If some decided that no attempt could be made against MALAKOFF FARM until the Quarry and COLOGNE FARM were in our hands and orders were issued forth taking Quarry and	See Appendix XII
		9.0pm	Liaison with 7th WORCESTERS established and orders exchanged. Arrangements were made with 295th Bde R.F.A. for artillery support.	
		11.0pm	Message received from Bde informing us that the Germans were reported to be returning on the Hindenburg line. Patrols sent out to confirm this.	
- do -	11.4.17	3.0am	Patrols reported the Quarry and farms in vicinity of COLOGNE FARM to be clear of the enemy and orders for attack were at once issued to company commanders. The artillery support was cancelled. A heavy engagement ensued as these places were found to be strongly held. An account of the battle is found in Appendix XIII	See Appendix XIII
		4.30am	The attacking troops retired to the original line held. Casualties. Officers Killed. Capt. T. BRYANT. Lieut. J.S.SIMONS. Lieut J.H. SHREWSBURY. " Wounded. Lieut. R.W. ALSTON. " wounded/captured. Lieut. R.W. ALSTON. " missing. J.W. WALKER. (K) Other ranks Killed. wounded and missing 254.	
		8.30pm	Relief. company reliefs. A Coy by D Coy. C Coy by B Coy. A+C coys suffered most formed into 2 composite company in reserve	

Army Form C. 2118.

WAR DIARY
or
INTELLIGENCE SUMMARY

(Erase heading not required.)

References to FRANCE Sheet 62 c S.E.

Place	Date	Hour	Summary of Events and Information	Remarks and references to Appendices
HARGICOURT	11.4.17	9.0 p.m.	Situation unchanged. Our lines were continuously shelled by the enemy today by Field Artillery and also by 15 cm Howitzers. We suffered a few casualties. 1 man killed 5 wounded. Attempts to establish a post at L.5.c.5.1. were met by heavy M.G. and rifle fire. A German post at L.5.a.9.5. was found to be strongly wired and held. Few	
— do —	12.4.17	5. a.m.	Considerable sniping was being carried on from enemy lines making movement of our patrols difficult. H.Q. were unmoved while on patrols.	
			Our dispositions unchanged. Communications with 7th WORCESTERS on left and 2/4 LEICESTERS on right was maintained. Our line was extended to embrace the German front as far as L.10.b.9.0. with a post at L.10.b.9.1.	
		2.5 p.m.	Lieut. F. WRIGHT killed while on patrol by sniper.	
— do —	13.4.17	8.0 a.m.	Sniping posts established in HARGICOURT by no movement in enemy lines was considerably depressed and their sniping practically ceased.	
			Our dispositions unchanged.	
— do —	14.4.17	8.0 a.m.	Dispositions unchanged. Our lines and Headquarters were shelled intermittently by day and night. Communication trenches were sunk or flanks. Posts were deepened and wire strengthened during the night. Steel shit and shelters were dug.	
		9.30 p.m.	A-C company relieved B coy in the left. D company being strongest arranged its own relief within the company. B coy in reserve at the Quarry in L.4.d.	
— do —	15.4.17	3.0 a.m.	Dispositions unchanged. A small post was dug during the night at L.5.a.5.6. but not held during the day.	
		10.0 p.m.	VILLERET attacked and captured on own right by 5 LEICESTERS south of our lines was established.	
— do —	16.4.17		Dispositions unchanged. Our patrols report the Quarry in L.5.d. and COLOGNE FARM to be held by enemy.	

Army Form C. 2118.

WAR DIARY
or
INTELLIGENCE SUMMARY
(Erase heading not required.)

Map. Ref. to Sheet. FRANCE Sheet 62° N.E. & S.E.

Place	Date	Hour	Summary of Events and Information	Remarks and references to Appendices
HARGICOURT.	17.4.17	—	Dispositions unchanged. B. Coy relieved A. C Coy on the left. A & C Coys Support at Quarry on L.4.d. Communication established with 2/4 LINCOLNS on right and OXON & BUCKS on left.	Yes
— do —	18.4.17		Dispositions unchanged. Enemy artillery was active during day and night shelling front line and Headquarters.	Yes. See Appendix XIV.
— do —	19.4.17	10.0 pm	Relief by 2/6th SHERWOOD FORESTERS completed. The Bn. marches back to VRAIGNES to rest billets. No lieut company arriving 4.0 am 20.4.17	Yes
VRAIGNES.	20.4.17		Working parties furnished for road scraping and repairing. Remainder of men cleaning & bathing.	Yes
— do —	21.4.17		Working parties for roads. Divison Economy for remainder of battalion.	Yes
— do —	22.4.17		All battalion on working parties.	Yes
— do —	23.4.17		Training commenced. Following officers have joined for duty.	
			Lieut. C.O.R. JACOB. 1st DEVONSHIRE RGT. 21.4.17	
			2 Lieut F.S. ROGERS. 4th DORSETSHIRE RGT. 21.4.17	
			" AKHURST 2nd DEVONSHIRE RGT 21.4.17	
			" R.J. BROOKE 4th NORFOLK REGT. 22.4.17	
			" A BEGG ditto. 22.4.17	
— do —	23 24.4.17	9.30 pm	Gas Alert ordered to be on.	Yes
— do —	24.4.17	—	Training continued. Bombers, Rifle Grenadiers, Lewis Gunners are being trained to meet good losses. A draft to supply required as Trench Strength in iron about 350 R.	Yes
		2.30 pm	Gas Alert taken off.	

Army Form C. 2118.

WAR DIARY
or
INTELLIGENCE SUMMARY

(Erase heading not required.)

Instructions regarding War Diaries and Intelligence Summaries are contained in F. S. Regs., Part II. and the Staff Manual respectively. Title Pages will be prepared in manuscript.

Map References to FRANCE Sheets 62c and 62b

Place	Date	Hour	Summary of Events and Information	Remarks and references to Appendices
VRAIGNES	25-4-17 to 28-4-17		Training continued. Working parties were found for road repairing. Instruction given in bombing, rifle grenade work, open warfare attack formations also practised. Instruction given in formations given in Offence-pamphlet S.S. 1919. The Bn. was inspected by the G.O.C. 59th Division who expressed himself as well satisfied with the appearance of the men.	
VRAIGNES	28-4-17	6.0 pm	Bn. moved off to relieve 2/5th N. STAFFORD REGT. in the right sub sector of the Divisional Area. Headquarters near LE VERGUIER.	Appendix XIII
LE VERGUIER	28-4-17	11.55 pm	Relief reported complete with no untoward happenings. Our dispositions are as follows. Right company – front line – "C" Coy. Holds a line of six posts extending from G.32.c.2.6. to G.32.a.1.1. with Lewis guns in centre. Right & left posts. Each post 1 NCO + 5 men. Support line from a trench running from R.6.a.?.5. to L.36.c.3.1. Each post 1 NCO + 3 men. Coy. H.Q at R.5.d.9.5. Left Company – front line – "B" Coy. An advanced post at G.31.a.5.4. garrisoned by 1 Officer + 24 men with Lewis guns. Support line of 3 posts between L.36.a.5.3. and L.36.a.5.0. Each post 1 NCO and 4 men. Lewis guns at extreme left post. Coy H.Q at R.5.6.4.7.	

2449 Wt. W14957/Mg0 750,000 1/16 J.B.C. & A. Forms/C.2118/12.

Army Form C. 2118.

WAR DIARY
or
INTELLIGENCE SUMMARY

(Erase heading not required.)

Map References to FRANCE Sheet 62c and 62b

Place	Date	Hour	Summary of Events and Information	Remarks and references to Appendices
	28.4.17		(Dispositions: B(?))	
			Right Support Company holding old German trench from R.5.a.3.3 to R.5.a.4.4 &	
			D'Coy. with 6 posts alternately Lewis Gun & Rifle posts Each	
			Post 1 NCO & 5 men	
			Coy. HQ and 1 platoon at R.5.a.6.1	
			Left Support Company 'A' Coy. holding old German trench from R.5.a.0.4. to L.34.b.1.8. with 1 Officer & 32 NCOs & men.	
			and also following posts	
			L.34.b.1.3. Lewis Gun 1 NCO & 6 men	
			L.34.b.0.3. Rifle do	
			L.34.b.0.1. Lewis Gun do	
			L.34.a.1.7. Rifle do	
			Battalion Headquarters established at L.33.d.2.5.	
			Communication was established with 20th LANCASHIRE FUSILIERS at G.32.c.2.5. and with 2/5th Bn. LEICESTERSHIRE REGT at G.95.d.3.4.	
			Two companies of the Battalion in support at JEANCOURT came up nightly to work on main line of resistance which is the line held by the Support companies of the unit as set out above	
LE VERGUIER	29.4.17 to 30.4.17		Dispositions maintained as for 28.4.17. Lieut E.G. AKHURST was wounded in advanced post at G.34.a.5.4. on 29.4.17. All improved posts and shell were dug on working parties at night	

Army Form C. 2118.

WAR DIARY
or
INTELLIGENCE SUMMARY
(Erase heading not required.)

Instructions regarding War Diaries and Intelligence Summaries are contained in F. S. Regs., Part II and the Staff Manual respectively. Title Pages will be prepared in manuscript.

FRANCE
Map Reference to Sheet. 62c and 62b

Place	Date	Hour	Summary of Events and Information	Remarks and references to Appendices
	(cont'd)		the advanced posts at G.31.a.5.4. Wire strengthened & extended in front line posts and main line of resistance. Enemy's shelling was desultory during these two days. Gas alert was ordered, the men being in a dangerous quarter (M E)	
Le VERGUIER	30.4.17		The following Officers have joined:—	
			2/Lieut. G. HOULDEN 8 Sth LINCOLNSHIRE RGT joined 26.4.17	
			2/Lieut C.J. HOOPER 4th (Res) DORSETSHIRE RGT. joined 29.4.17	
			" R.C. INGRAM 3rd. DEVONSHIRE REGT. " "	
			" R. DO GOOD 4th Res DORSETSHIRE RGT. " "	
			Situation very quiet the whole day.	

W.H.M May
Lieut Colonel
Cmdg 2/5 Lincolnshire Regt

Map. Ref. to
FRANCE. Sheet.
62° N.E.

Account of the Operation carried out by the 2/5th Bn.
LINCOLNSHIRE REGT on night 10/11 April 1917.

APPENDIX XIII

9th April 1917

1. Situation previous to Operations

The 2/4 LINCOLN Regt. held a line of posts running N & S about 800 yds W. of HARGICOURT with a patrol at the western edge of the village. The 2/5 LINCOLN Regt at ROISEL were ordered to move to TEMPLEUX and at night attack the German position South of HARGICOURT and occupy the German trenches from L.11a.8.6. to FERVAQUE FARM.

Before this could be done the Germans evacuated their trenches and took up positions along a line MALAKOFF FARM, COLOGNE FARM, the QUARRY in L.5.d. VILLERET with advanced posts in the trench running from Eastern edge of HARGICOURT to MALAKOFF FARM.

The 2/5 LINCOLN REGT established posts at L.4.b.9.4 & L.5.c.4.3. L.4.d.8.1. L.11.a.3.6 and L.11.a.6.4 with supports in SUNKEN ROAD at L.4.9.9.2 & road at L.4.d.2.1. & Quarry at L.4.C.2.4.
Repeated attempts were made to occupy Pt. L.11.a.8.6. & to bomb down the trench to MALAKOFF FARM but these were frustrated my M.G. fire from the QUARRY in L.5.d, the trench at this point being very shallow & offering no cover.

Communications were established with 2/4 LEICESTERS on right and 7th WORCESTERS on left.

10th April 1917

Dispositions unchanged. Orders were issued to O.C. A Coy on night to again attempt to bomb down the enemy trench towards MALAKOFF FARM.

2. The Operations of the night 10/11 April 1917.

5.15.pm. Following message received from 177th Infy Bde.

"144th Bde will this evening commence to
"establish itself on the high ground about F.29.b
"F.29.d. F.17.b & F.17.d. including X roads F.29.b.0.3.
"You will get into touch with Bn on your left
"and take every opportunity of pushing forward
"to the German trench from L.11.b.1.4. to
"MALAKOFF FARM. aaa. COLOGNE FARM and the
"QUARRY in L.5.d should also be taken and
"the position as soon as taken should be
"consolidated. aaa. Say if you require
"artillery support and on what objective &
"at what time.

9.50 pm. Our Liason Officer returned from Bn on our left with copy of their orders for attack. Owing to short time permission was obtained to arrange artillery support direct and Operation Order No.   was issued to companies and F.O.O. of 295th Bde R.F.A. The Zero hour for attack was 4.30 am. 11.4.17 to coincide with attack of 144 Brigade on our left

2

10th April 1917.

10.30 p.m. Two messages were received from 177th Inf Bde.
1. Stating that 48th Division reported enemy retiring back to HINDENBURG LINE & directing that patrols be sent out to verify this.
2. Asking if we had yet occupied enemy trench running towards MALAKOFF FARM. If not what steps were being taken to do so tonight.

Patrols were sent out to the QUARRY in L.5.d and in direction of MALAKOFF FARM

11th April 1917
2.30 a.m. Patrols reported that the Quarry and the neighborhood of MALAKOFF FARM & E end of HARGICOURT was clear of the enemy

It then appeared that taking these reports in conjunction with the message 1 above, that we should seize the Quarry & COLOGNE FARM and consolidate the enemy trench running from HARGICOURT to MALAKOFF FARM.

Verbal orders were at once issued to this effect A company to take the Quarry and C Company the left with COLOGNE FARM. The artillery preparation was cancelled and the attacking companies informed that on sending up the S.O.S. signal a barrage would be put along a line drawn between VILLERET and the Quarry in L.5.d

4.0 a.m. A Company formed up for the attack on a 2 platoon frontage with 2 waves to each platoon, bombers & riflemen extended 3 paces in front wave Lewis guns in second wave Supporting platoons moved in small columns of about a section. A heavy enemy barrage was laid down about them but casualties were few at this stage and the formation adopted seems to have been quite suitable. The attack was launched from S.W. corner of Square L.11.b and made direct for the quarry. The enemy appears to have been surprised and many dugouts were bombed along the road passing S.E. of the Quarry as shown on the map. The Quarry is of much greater extent than is shown on the official map and the platoons on entering made good progress capturing about 40 prisoners which could not subsequently be held. In the Quarry they were met by heavy rifle and M.G. fire and lost the Coy Commander Capt T. BRYANT who was killed in leading his men, encouraging them from the bank at the top of the Quarry. The machine guns were rushed in succession

11th April 1917 — by men lead by 2/Lt. M.T. CHAMBERS. In one case the German gunner stuck to his post & continued firing until shot by Lt. Chambers but the majority of the enemy seemed anxious to get away and the 2nd M.G. was abandoned. Our casualties had been somewhat heavy, - probably 40. 2nd Lieut. J.S SIMONS was wounded twice & had to withdraw, and the Quarry widened as the attack progressed, making the line very thin.

4.40am. The attacking coy in the Quarry was strongly counter attacked from the direction of VILLERET and being very much outnumbered was forced to retire to the positions held the previous night. This retirement was carried out in good order and a post with a Lewis gun was established at L.11.a 8.6.

The left company "C" Company formed up in similar formation and moved against the enemy trench running N through L.5.d and 5.6. The wire was cut and our bombing parties entered the trench and commenced bombing towards MALAKOFF FARM. They were almost immediately very strongly counterattacked from the direction of COLOGNE FARM by a force estimated at about 250 men. They appear to have been surrounded and mostly captured because very few men returned. No clear idea of what had actually happened could be obtained. The remnant of the company were withdrawn to the posts held the previous night. Lieuts. R.W. ALSTON & J.W. WALKER were reported missing. 2/Lieut. J.H. SHREWSBURY was wounded.

Our total casualties among Other ranks were 254 killed wounded and missing. No estimate can be given of the enemy's casualties but they could not have been inconsiderable.

J.C. Ingram
Capt. Adjt.
1/5 Lincoln Regt.

13/4/17

Confidential

War Diary of
2/5 Bn. LINCOLNSHIRE Regt.
from 1/5/17 to 31/5/17

Vol 4

W. Muddley. Major
Comndg 2/5 Lincolnshire Regt.

1.6.17

ORIGINAL

SECRET

2/5 LINCOLNSHIRE REGT

Reference to France sheet 62b + 62c.

Army Form C. 2118.

WAR DIARY
INTELLIGENCE SUMMARY
(Erase heading not required.)

Instructions regarding War Diaries and Intelligence Summaries are contained in F.S. Regs., Part II. and the Staff Manual respectively. Title Pages will be prepared in manuscript.

Place	Date	Hour	Summary of Events and Information	Remarks and references to Appendices
Le VERGUIER	1/5/17.		Situation quiet. A new post was commenced at G.31.b.4.6 and was partially wired. The 20th Lancashire Fusiliers attacked the wood in G.32 central but did not take it. Our casualties were Nil. Fighting Strength of Battalion 29 Officers and 542 O.R. This included all details away from the unit. Our actual trench strength is 370 O.R. Nothing further.	
— do —	2/5/17.		Situation quiet. A new post was dug at G.31.b.8.5 to be held at night as a listening post. Lieut. C.O.R. JACOB has taken over command of B Company. Weather conditions much improved. 2/Lt. company reliefs carried out. D company relieving C company in the front line and A company relieving B. Capt. M. Fitzpatrick has taken over command of A Company D Coy now commanded by Capt. G.L. Hill.	See Attachment No XVI
— do —	3/5/17.		Situation normal. Our front line posts were shelled occasionally during the day & night. We suffered no casualties. The enemies shells experienced to have been 5.9 cm. New post dug G.31.b.6.4½ and the posts at G.31.b.7.2 extended and wire strengthened.	
— do —	4/5/17.		The following posts were taken over from the 7th Leicester Regiment on our left and occupied by B Coy during to a new allotment of Brigade Areas. G.31.c.2.8., G.25.d.3.4, L.30.c.9.7 forming extension of our front line. L.30.c.8.4. L.30.c.5.7 forming a support line. Company Headquarters L.30.c.2.3. traversed and wired.	See Attachment XVII
		8.30pm	The wire in front of our extreme right front post was cut down to allow the 23 Manchester Regt to pass through to attack the wood in G.32 centre. Their operations were successful.	

Army Form C. 2118.

WAR DIARY
INTELLIGENCE SUMMARY
(Erase heading not required.)

Instructions regarding War Diaries and Intelligence Summaries are contained in F. S. Regs., Part II. and the Staff Manual respectively. Title Pages will be prepared in manuscript.

References to France sheets 62d & 62c.

Place	Date	Hour	Summary of Events and Information	Remarks and references to Appendices
LE VERGUIER	5/5/17	6.0am	Situation normal, and remained so all day.	
		9.30pm	What appeared to be a German attack developed against our extreme right post. As the enemy seemed to number about 200 an S.O.S. rocket was sent up and our artillery put a barrage in front. At the same time our machine guns opened fire, and the Lewis guns and riflemen in our front line post. The enemy did not reach our front line, and it would appear that part of his attacking troops had lost direction and caught our extreme right. His main attack at any rate was on the wood in G.32.central which was captured by him and subsequently retaken by the 20th Lancashire Fusiliers on our right. We suffered no casualties.	see Appendix XVIII
— do —	6/5/17	—	Relieved by 94 LINCOLN REGT. when we took over in reserve to 94 LINCOLNS.	see Appendix XIX
JEANCOURT	7/5/17 to 15/5/17	—	In support. Each night working parties of 2 companies stay in the main line of Resistance in the LE VERGUIER section. During the day the roads in the village were cleared and numerous heaps covered and burnt. Aeroplanes converts into the deep fly proof type. The village was occasionally shelled with 9.2 cm shells but we had no casualties. 2nd Lt J.H. GOULDBY joined the unit for duty from No. 9 I.B.D. on 14.5.17 from 4th (Res)/LINCOLNSHIRE REGT.	
— do —	15.5.17		Relieved by 25th Bn SHERWOOD FORESTERS. On relief the Battalion proceeded by march route to CARTIGNY and went under canvas there. The camp was situated at P.23.d.9.8.	

Army Form C. 2118.

WAR DIARY
or
INTELLIGENCE SUMMARY.
(Erase heading not required.)

Instructions regarding War Diaries and Intelligence Summaries are contained in F.S. Regs., Part II. and the Staff Manual respectively. Title pages will be prepared in manuscript.

References to Sheets 62 c. S.E. and 57 c. S.E. (1/20,000)

Hour, Date, Place	Summary of Events and Information	Remarks and references to Appendices
CARTIGNY 16/5/17. to 24/5/17	The battalion remained at CARTIGNY during this time and carried out training. The general subjects carried out were close order drill, bayonet fighting, gas helmet and box respirator practice, musketry and open and trench attack formations. At the same time specialist training was given in bombing, r/g grenades, Lewis gun, sniping and signalling. Afternoons were devoted to training games - of which there are large quantities - and games & recreational physical training. All equipment and stores were checked and deficiencies indented for.	JCW
do 25/5/17	Camp was struck at 5.45 am and the battalion proceeded by road route to a camp near EQUANCOURT - ⓡ starting at 8.0 am. The day was very hot and about 60 men fell out owing to the heat but all regained the battalion in camp during the afternoon and evening.	see Appendix XX
EQUANCOURT 26/5/17	Training continued. B.O. and company commanders proceeded to the front line at GOUZEAUCOURT WOOD preparatory to taking over.	JCW
do 27/5/17 8.0 pm	Bn moved up to GOUZEAUCOURT WOOD (P.22.a) in support to 2/5 LEICESTER REGT in front line. Distributed as follows.	see Appendix XXI

(73989) W4141—463. 400,000. 9/14. H.&J.Ltd. Forms/C. 2118/10.

Army Form C. 2118.

WAR DIARY
or
INTELLIGENCE SUMMARY

(Erase heading not required.)

Reference to Sheet France 57 c. S.E.

Instructions regarding War Diaries and Intelligence Summaries are contained in F.S. Regs., Part II. and the Staff Manual respectively. Title Pages will be prepared in manuscript.

Place	Date	Hour	Summary of Events and Information	Remarks and references to Appendices
GOUZEAUCOURT GOUZEAUCOURT WOOD	27/5/17	—	D. Company in the Intermediate line running through Q.17.b and Q.18.a. A Company in the "Brown" line running through Q.25.b and Q.29.a. B and C companies with Battalion Headquarters in GOUZEAUCOURT WOOD at Q.22.c.3.3.	
–do–	28/5/17	—	A and D companies were relieved by 9/4 LINCOLN REGIMENT and marched to GOUZEAUCOURT WOOD.	
–do–	28/5/17 and 29/5/17		The wood has been mainly the scenario so stakes and horse lines and large dumps of manure and refuse were carried over with earth. During the night working parties were sent up for the front line.	
–do–	30/5/17	9.15pm	The Bn moved up to take over the front line & intermediate lines in the left sub sector which the Brigade is now taking over. B company of the 4th E. LANCS. Rgt. in the front line. B company relieved the night company of the 4/5 Lincs & those LEICESTERS on the right, B company relieved the left company of 1/K 9/5 R. 4th LINCOLNS on the line. C and D companies relief completed at 1.10 am 31/5/17.	see Appendices XX.11
BEAUCAMP	31/5/17		Dispositions: Front line. Right company. B Coy holding front line trench from Q.12.b.7.0 to Q.12.b.0.3. In touch with 9/5 LEICESTER RGT on right. H.Q. Q.12.b.5.1. Left company A Coy holding front line trench from Q.12.b.0.3. to Q.12.a.6.5. Support companies in Intermediate line including trench from Q.15.a.3.2. Coy having from Q.18.d.0.3. to Q.18.a.3.9. and D company from Q.15.a.3.2 to Q.17.b.3.6. Bn. H.Q. Q.17.b.5.4. Touch maintained with 4th E. LANCS. Rgt on left front line and intermediate line.	

Army Form C. 2118.

WAR DIARY
or
INTELLIGENCE SUMMARY

(Erase heading not required.)

Place	Date	Hour	Summary of Events and Information	Remarks and references to Appendices
				References to Sheets France 57d SE (7)
BEAUCAMP	31/5/17	—	The situation has been very quiet. No offensive spirit has been shown by the enemy. Lieut MORRIS TONGE CHAMBERS has during the month been awarded the Military Cross, for gallantry in the action of 11th April 1917 at HARGICOURT (see account attached as appendix to war diary for April)	

W Wheadon Major
Comdg. 2/5 Bn. Lincolnshire Regt.

ORIGINAL — Army Form C. 2118.

SECRET

WAR DIARY
or
INTELLIGENCE SUMMARY
(Erase heading not required.)

CONFIDENTIAL

War Diary of the 2/5th Bn Lincolnshire Regt
from
1/6/17 to 30/6/17.

[signature]
Lieut. Colonel
Cmdg 2/5th Bn Lincoln Regt.

Army Form C. 2118.

WAR DIARY
or
INTELLIGENCE SUMMARY
(Erase heading not required.)

Map Reference. France Sheet 57c. S.E. 2&0.0.

Place	Date	Hour	Summary of Events and Information	Remarks and references to Appendices
BEAUCAMP	1/6/17	—	Fighting Strength. 31 Officers 543 O.R. Of these, 6 Officers and 92 other ranks are absent from the unit for various causes. A draft of 50 O.R. was received to-day and one officer. Lieut. W.G. FENTON. Working parties worked during the night on the front line trenches - which were in bad condition and very shallow. They are in front and strengthened and extended. Fly proof latrine were made in front line & Intermediate line trenches. Three advanced posts to hold a garrison of 1 officer & 12 O.R. and a L.G. were dug at Q.12.b.9.6, Q.12.b.1.7 and Q.12.a.8.5. The posts were not deep enough to hold by day. Lieut. G.J. PEARSON and 2 O.R. were wounded while on patrol. The patrol appears to have met a German patrol in front of our line. The wounds were caused by bombs.	
—do—	2/6/17	—	The enemy shelled BEAUCAMP and trenches in neighborhood killing 1 O.R. and wounding 2 with shrapnel. Shelling was very desultory. The working parties at night were harassed by enemy machine-gun fire. It was found that responses from our Lewis Guns kept the machine guns quiet. The enemy shows very little activity in this sector and only one patrol has so far been encountered. Front line trenches work on advanced posts continued. Mine crafts. A Support line is being dug about 100x N. of BEAUCAMP and a new communication trench to Intermediate line via W.edge of BEAUCAMP. A communication trench is also being dug from Intermediate line at Q.18.a.6.0 to night Battalion H.Q. at Q.18.a.9.8. The 1/4th E.LANCS on our left have been relieved by the 9/6th SHERWOOD FORESTERS who have taken over an extended.	Jer

2449 Wt. W14957/M90 750,000 1/16 J.B.C. & A. Forms/C.2118/12.

Army Form C. 2118.

WAR DIARY
or
INTELLIGENCE SUMMARY
(Erase heading not required.)

Instructions regarding War Diaries and Intelligence Summaries are contained in F. S. Regs., Part II. and the Staff Manual respectively. Title Pages will be prepared in manuscript.

Map reference France Sheet 57c S.E. 20303

Place	Date	Hour	Summary of Events and Information	Remarks and references to Appendices
BEAUCAMP	3/6/17	-	Enemy shells intermittent line at intervals wounding 2 O.R. Shelling was very irregular & few shells. The left hand post at Q.12.a.8.8. today hands over to 7th SHERWOOD FORESTERS being in their area. A new post was commenced at Q.12.6.5.F. Posts numbered from right to left. No.1. Q.12.b.9.6. No.2 Q.12.b.5.8 No.3 Q.12.a.1.7	See appendix XXI
BEAUCAMP	4/6/17	-	Nos 1 and 3 are now held by day with 1 Officer and work on front line and communication trenches continued. Gun 130 O.R. minimal today. A relief by D Coy B Coy relieved by C Coy. Enemy quiet all day. Work continued at night. No O.R. post known yet for holding by day.	See appendix XXI
-do-	5/6/17	-	Enemy shelled intermediate line at intervals wounding 3. O.R. Only a few shells were sent over and a large percentage were "duds". Work continued as before.	
-do-	6/6/17	-	Situation unchanged. No enemy patrols have been encountered. Our patrols report work being carried on at the line of enemy rifle pits running some 500 yards beyond our advanced posts.	
-do-	7/6/17	-	Bn relieved by 7th Lincolnshire Regiment. Relief passed off without event. Bn. going all day. Bn. relief (In process) to GOUZEAUCOURT WOOD acting as Battalion in Support.	See appendix XXII
GOUZEAUCOURT WOOD	8/6/17 to 17/6/17	-	Battalion in Support. Defence scheme issued in attached showing disposition of companies etc. During this time working parties were found each night to work on the communication trenches and front line system Shelters were dug and constructed	See appendix XXIII

2449 Wt. W14957/M90 750,000 1/16 J.B.C. & A. Forms/C.2118/12.

Army Form C. 2118.

WAR DIARY
or
INTELLIGENCE SUMMARY

(Erase heading not required.)

Map Ref. France Sheet 57c. S.E. 1/20,000.

Place	Date	Hour	Summary of Events and Information	Remarks and references to Appendices
GOUZEAUCOURT WOOD	3/6/17 to 17/6/17	—	In the Brown Line. Lt Colonel M.E. Raffey resumes and assumes command on 7/9/17	See Appendix XXIV
— do —	17/6/17	10.0 p.m	The Battalion relieved the 7/4th Bn Lincolnshire Regt in the Brigade left sub sector Relief was carried out without interruption. The relief Battalion entered the front line posts considerably, another as now an almost continuous trench between the posts at Q.12.6.4.3 and Q.6.d.2.0. The line of front end posts to now the Main Line of resistance and is to be held at all costs. Work was commenced on the trench proposed between the posts at Q.12.6.9.5 and Q.12.6.4.3, and about 200 yards completed. A new post was established at Q.12.6.4.3. Dispositions as follows:— 'B' Coy. Right front line with posts at Q.12.6.9.5 and Q.12.6.7.7. 9 1 Officer 18 O.R. each and 1 Lewis Gun. Remainder of company in Support line from Q.12.6.7.0 to Q.12.6.1.4. Company H.Q. Q.12.6.6.M. 2 Lewis guns in support line. 'A' Coy. Left front line with posts at Q.12.6.4.3. and Q.6.d.2.0 each of 1 officer 24 O.R. and 1 Lewis Gun each. Remainder of company in support line from Q.12.6.1.4 to Q.12.a.6.5. Company H.Q. & C.T. at Q.12.a.7.3. 'C' Coy. reserve line from Q.12.d.2.6 to Q.12.c.2.9. with 3 Lewis Reserve company 2 in reserve. Guns. Bn HQ and Headquarters company in Sunken road at Q.12.d.6.0. 'D' Coy were accommodated in the 2 Tunnel stair line in rear reserve. Communication was established by patrol with the 176th Rjants Brigade on our left and with the 4/5th Bn Leicestershire Regt on our right.	

Army Form C. 2118.

WAR DIARY
or
INTELLIGENCE SUMMARY

(Erase heading not required.)

Instructions regarding War Diaries and Intelligence Summaries are contained in F.S. Regs., Part II. and the Staff Manual respectively. Title Pages will be prepared in manuscript.

Map Ref. France Sheet 57 C. S.E. 1/20,000

Place	Date	Hour	Summary of Events and Information	Remarks and references to Appendices
BEAUCAMP.	18/6/17	—	Enemy quiet all day. Work continued at night on joining up the front line bays to make a continuous trench. The trench between Nos. 1 Post and Post No. 1A is continuous but not complete. 300' of trench again dying between No. 1 Post and the left post of the unit on our right. There are about 200' to be dug between posts 1A and 2. Shelters and dug outs latrines are being constructed to the trenches as dug. Enemy machine guns and snipers were fairly active during the night, but it is known that they are nearly silenced by Lewis gun fire from the covering parties. The enemy has shown little offensive spirit although he has been twice seen from the post next R.G. our listening patrols hear enemy working parties on the line of rifle pits running through O.1 and R.C. from an photos this appears to be an almost continuous trench.	Jey
— do —	19/6/17	—	Situation unchanged. Enemy quiet by day. Work was continued at night on front line trenches. The trench between No. 1 Post and the trench on our right was commenced and 300' more dug. Its 2 feet. Posts 1A and 2 are almost joined by continuous trench. About 100' yet.	Jey
— do —	20/6/17	1.30 a.m	A German patrol advanced against No. 3 Post and was challenged by our sentry group. On them on receiving no answer opened fire and the enemy pistol retired leaving one slightly wounded prisoner in our hands.	Jey
		6.0 p.m	Situation unchanged. A few 77 m.m shells were sent over by the enemy but we suffered no casualties.	
		—	Work continued at night. There is now continuous trench along the whole of our front and also between ourselves another Bn to 75 Brigade Posts on our right. The wire was strengthened and entries in front of Nos. 1 and 3 Posts.	Jey

Army Form C. 2118.

WAR DIARY
or
INTELLIGENCE SUMMARY
(Erase heading not required.)

Maps Ref FRANCE. Sheet 57 c S.E. 1/20,000.

Place	Date	Hour	Summary of Events and Information	Remarks and references to Appendices
BEAUCAMP.	21/6/17	—	Enemy quiet all day. Bn. relieved by 2/4th Bn. SHERWOOD FORESTERS. Relief passed off quietly. Bn. moved into Divisional reserve at EQUANCOURT and bivouaced at G.W. V.11.a.3.3.	See Appendix XXV JCH
EQUANCOURT.	22/6/17 to 30/6/17	—	Training carried on. 236 men fired a short course Musketry on 30 yards range. Lewis Gun firing and bombing instruction were also carried out. "D" Company were absent during this time on a musketry course at 4th Army Schools.	JCH

J. M. Field
1/7/17.

H. M. Mapp
Lieut Colonel
Comdg 2/5 Lincolnshire Regt.

2/5th Lincolnshire Regt.
Defence Scheme for Support Battalion
177th Infantry Brigade

Ref France Sheet 57. S.E.

1. **Distribution** — On receipt of alarm

    (a) 'A' Coy will occupy the BROWN LINE 2 platoons from Brigade Right Boundary to Q28 central and 2 platoons from Q27 b7.7 to Bde Left Boundary. This company will remain in the BROWN LINE.

    (b) B, C and D Coys will proceed independently to the Intermediate line and will occupy as follows:—

    'B' Coy from R19a 0.7 to Q18d 0.5 (road inclusive)
    'C' "   "   Q18d 0.5 (road exclusive) to Q18a 2.6
    'D' "   "   Q18a 2.6 to Q17b 1.8.

    Coy. Commdrs. will ensure that all officers and N.C.O° down to platoon sergeants know their exact positions in the Intermediate line, and the way to them both by day and night.

2. **HEADQUARTERS.** Bn H.Q and R.A.P. will be at Q17d 5.3.

3. **COMMUNICATIONS.** Signalling Officer will utilize the existing line from Bde H.Q to Q17b 9.5 and will run out lines from Bn H.Q to H.Q of B. C and D Coys. Communication with A Coy will be by runner.

4. **SAA GRENADES.** 100 rounds additional S.A.A. will be carried by each man. The coy reserve of grenades will be carried taken up with Companies.

5. **WORKING PARTIES.** In case of alarm during the night when Companies are out on working parties they will at once proceed to their respective trenches.

   As much S.A.A and bombs as possible will be carried up by the Company H.Q. personnel and carrying parties will be sent back for remaining S.A.A bombs and Lewis Guns.

10/6/17.

Capt & Adjt
2/5 Lincoln Regt.

WAR DIARY or INTELLIGENCE SUMMARY

Army Form C. 2118.

Vol 6

CONFIDENTIAL

War Diary of 2/5th Bn. the
LINCOLNSHIRE REGT
from
1st July 1917 to 31st July 1917

M.M.Moffey Lieut Colonel
Cmdg 2/5th Bn Lincoln R

Army Form C. 2118.

WAR DIARY
or
INTELLIGENCE SUMMARY

(Erase heading not required.)

Map Reference - France Sheet 57 C S.E. 1/20,000

Place	Date	Hour	Summary of Events and Information	Remarks and references to Appendices
NEUVILLE.	1-7-17 to 5-7-17	—	The Bn moved by march route from EQUANCOURT to NEUVILLE becoming battalion in Brigade Reserve in the Bihem Sector (left sector 59th Divisional Front.) Bn H.Q. were at P.22.d.5.7 and the battalion was accomodated in tents and shelters in the vicinity. During this period the battalion found working parties by day and night on the communication trenches in the Brigade Sector.	See appendix
— do —	5-7-17		The battalion relieved the 2/4th LINCOLNSHIRE REGT. in the trenches of the right sub-sector 59th Division Front. The relief passed off without event. Dispositions of the Battalion were as follows — Right front line. D. Coy - 3 platoons in front line trench from Q.6.d.10. to Q.6.c.3.2. 1 " " Support line trench from Q.12.a.9.5 to Q.12.a.0.7 Coy H.Q. Q.11.d.3.7. Left front line C Coy - 2 " " " " " Q.6.c.3.2 to Q.5.d.8.2. 2 " " front " " " " Coy H.Q. Q.11.b.4.6. Support Company. A. Coy - 4 platoons in trench from Q.12.a.7.3 to Q.11.b.4.6. Coy H.Q. Q.11.d.8.7. Reserve Company B Coy 2 platoons in trench Q.11.d.8.7 to Q.11.c.5.9. 2 " " " " Q.17.a.9.6 to Q.16.b.7.6. Coy. H.Q. Q.17.b.1.6. Battalion H.Q. Q.17.b.2.6. Trench strength of Bn was 21 Officers and 500 O.R. The 2/5th Bn. SHERWOOD FORESTERS were on our right and the 2/5th Bn. LEICESTERSHIRE REGT on the right.	See appendix

WAR DIARY or INTELLIGENCE SUMMARY

Army Form C. 2118.

(Erase heading not required.)

Map Reference. FRANCE SHEET 57 c S.E.

Place	Date	Hour	Summary of Events and Information	Remarks and references to Appendices
BEAUCAMP	6-7-17		Situation quiet. Our patrols have encountered no enemy patrols in No man's land. Work was continued on improvement of trenches. The front line trenches are very shallow, in some places not more than 2 feet. Wire on the left company frontage is good but requires thickening which was commenced tonight. A high double apron wire commenced on the night. A patrol of 1 Officer and 25 men was sent out to occupy BOARS COPSE (P.b.6.c) and the remains went off it. They encountered no enemy and returned at 2.30 am, leaving a party of 1 NCO and 6 men to remain in the copse by day.	
— do —	7-7-17 to 9-7-17		Work was continued on the trenches and the front line was taken down to 5'6" and fire steps dug in the tumps. A complete double apron fence was constructed along the night company front. The patrol of 1 Officer & 25 men were sent out to BOARS COPSE on the nights of 7th & 8th and met with no enemy. On the night of the 9th the day standing patrol of 1 NCO & 5 men which had been in BOARS COPSE through the day, withdrew before the night patrol got out, and met the nearest of the enemy. As the battalion occupied the copse and refused it so as to have for a raid on our own trenches not to handicap the copse were in process of being relieved by the London Regt it was decided not to hand over the inevitable retaliation on our trenches would cause many casualties. The trenches & so the inevitable retaliation on our trenches. Transport should have initiative in the copse might last full of men and many patrols, transport showed little initiative in the copse. The officer in charge of the night patrol sighted 4 of the enemy and stalked it. The relief passed off without further event. The front line companies were relieved by the 2/7th LONDON REGT and the H.Q. and intermediate line in D7 b + a by the 3/5th LONDON REGT.	
	10-7-17		The battalion marched from trenches to EQUANCOURT arriving about 5.0 am. Accommodated in canvas camp. Was struck at 9.0 a.m. and the Battalion proceeded by march route to BARASTRE being accommodated under canvas on D.16.d. (Map ref FRANCE, SHEET 57 c. S.W. 1/20000)	

Army Form C. 2118.

WAR DIARY
or
INTELLIGENCE SUMMARY
(Erase heading not required.)

Instructions regarding War Diaries and Intelligence Summaries are contained in F.S. Regs., Part II. and the Staff Manual respectively. Title Pages will be prepared in manuscript.

Place	Date	Hour	Summary of Events and Information	Remarks and references to Appendices
BARASTRE	1-7-17 31-7-17		Battalion carried out training. The chief subjects being, Trench to Trench attack by Battalion, Brigade and Division. Musketry; firing on 30 yards range and field firing range. Lewis gun firing. Bayonet fighting. Physical Exercises. Instruction given to in Bombing, rifle Grenades, runners, stretcher bearers, Scouts and Snipers. Sports and games were encouraged among the men and an hours recreational training was carried out each day. Leave to England commenced during the month.	
	1-8-17			

R. M. Murphy
Lieut Colonel
Comdg 2/5th B. Lincolnshire Regt

ORIGINAL Army Form C. 2118.

WAR DIARY
or
INTELLIGENCE SUMMARY
(Erase heading not required.)

Vol 7

CONFIDENTIAL.

War Diary of the 2/5th Bn. Lincolnshire Regt.

from 1/8/17.

to 31/8/17.

Walker Lt Colonel
Commdg. 2/5th Bn Lincolnshire Regt.

Army Form C. 2118.

WAR DIARY
or
INTELLIGENCE SUMMARY

(Erase heading not required.)

SECRET

2/5 Lincoln Regt. August 1917

Instructions regarding War Diaries and Intelligence Summaries are contained in F. S. Regs, Part II. and the Staff Manual respectively. Title Pages will be prepared in manuscript.

Place	Date	Hour	Summary of Events and Information	Remarks and references to Appendices
BARASTRE (O.16.d)	1/8/17 to 21/8/17		MAP. REF. FRANCE Sheet $\left\{\begin{array}{l}57^c \text{ S.W.} \\ 57^d \text{ S.E.}\end{array}\right.$ $\frac{1}{20,000}$ During the period the battalion was in training. # Trench to trench attack extensively practiced by companies, battalion, brigade, and Division. Open warfare similarly. Much attention has also been paid to individual instruction in bombing, rifle grenades, Lewis Gun ors in the training of runners, scouts and snipers, signallers etc. The battalion is better + in the respects than it has ever been previously. The following officers joined in the date shewn. 2/Lt E.S. HINTON - 11/8/17 Capt H.M. Newsum 16/7/17 " S. PLOWMAN " " E.W. GARRAD - 12/8/17 " W.H. MORRIS - 12/8/17	
HEDAUVILLE (P.34c)	21-8-17		Bn moved to HEDAUVILLE. As usual battalion marches half way fell had battalion travels half way in motor lorries. They had a short change over. Accomodated in huts etc in village.	
- do -	22-8-17 to 30-8-17		Training continued. Route marching, and individual instruction as above. Special Mention was paid to platoon attacks against single posts(as strong points. This in view of the role the Division is expected to play in the new area.	
BRIELE (Belgium) France Sheet 27 1/40,000 J.10.b.	31-8-17		Bn moves by staff train to BRIELE entraining at ALBERT detraining at PROVEN. Accomodated in Bn B.	

WAR DIARY
INTELLIGENCE SUMMARY

Army Form C. 2118.

Place	Date	Hour	Summary of Events and Information	Remarks and references to Appendices
BRIELEN (J.10.b)	31/5/17		Map ref. Belgium France Sheet 27 1/40000	
			Following drafts have been received during the month	
			1/5/17 128 O.R. ⎫	
			12/5/17 5 O.R. ⎬ General Physique & training – good	
			18/5/17 52 O.R. ⎭	
			19/5/17 14 O.R. ⎫ Lacking in individual training e.g. Lewis gun, bombing	
			24/5/17 20 O.R. ⎬ rifle grenade, signalling.	
			31/5/17 2/Lieut W.J. GALE ⎫ from 3rd LINCOLNS	
			" K.A.S. FOWLER ⎭	
			Strength 41 bn. 37 Officers, 951 O.R.	

M.M.M.K?
Lieut. Colonel
Cmdg. 7th Bn Lincolnshire Regt.

WAR DIARY
INTELLIGENCE SUMMARY
(Erase heading not required.)

Army Form C. 2118.

CONFIDENTIAL.

War Diary of the 2/5th Batt. The Lincolnshire Regt.
from 1/9/17 to 30/9/17.

H.M.Bray Lt. Col.
Commdg 2/5th Lincoln Regt.

Confidential

Army Form C. 2118.

WAR DIARY
INTELLIGENCE SUMMARY
(Erase heading not required.)

Instructions regarding War Diaries and Intelligence Summaries are contained in F.S. Regs., Part II. and the Staff Manual respectively. Title Pages will be prepared in manuscript.

SEPTEMBER

Map Refs. France & Belgium Sheet 27. 1/40,000 1/40,000
France + Belgium Sheet 28

Place	Date	Hour	Summary of Events and Information	Remarks and references to Appendices
NINNEZEELE (J.27)	1/9/17 to 20/9/17		In Camp at J.10 Central (Sheet 27). Batt accommodated in tents. Training continued, chiefly practice of attack formations against concrete blockhouses. Individual training in bombing, signalling, scouting, Lewis Gunnery was also carried out.	Yes
HILHOEK (L.15.b.4.6.) Sheet 27	21/9/17 to 23/9/17		In Camp at L.15.d.2.0 (Sheet 27). Accommodated in tents. Training on above lines continued.	Yes
GOLDFISH CHATEAU H.11 Central (Sheet 28)	23/9/17 to 24/9/17		In Camp at Huts 5.3 under Canvas. Awaiting orders to proceed up the line. Actual attack practice carried out with objectives marked out to correspond with objectives to be actually attacked.	Yes
ST. JEAN (C.27.d) Sheet 28	24/9/17	10.0 p.m.	Moved to ST. JEAN. The Bn was accommodated in trenches in the area S. of WEILTJE.	Yes
	25/9/17		The CO Adjutant and Company Commanders taking part in the attack reconnoitred the ground on which the attack was to be made. Our objectives could not be seen owing to mist, and to the fact that the whole of Hill 37 was not in our hands. The position of HQ and point of assembly were marked down.	
- do -		2.0 p.m.	Operation orders issued. The whole operation has been previously discussed many times with officers but the issue of orders was delayed pending the receipt of information as to place of assembly.	
- do -		11.0 p.m.	Bn moved forward to place of assembly. Bn Battle HQ: IBERION (D.19.b.22) (Sheet 28)	Yes

Confidential

Army Form C. 2118.

WAR DIARY
or
INTELLIGENCE SUMMARY
(Erase heading not required.)

MAP. REF. FRANCE & BELGIUM Sheets 27 N.W. and N.E.

Instructions regarding War Diaries and Intelligence Summaries are contained in F. S. Regs., Part II. and the Staff Manual respectively. Title Pages will be prepared in manuscript.

Place	Date	Hour	Summary of Events and Information	Remarks and references to Appendices
W.H.Hill 37	26/9/17	—	For account of operations see Appendix. Jurnes and held its objectives. The battalion attacked.	
—do—	—do—	—	The night 26-27 passed quietly and no attempt was made by the enemy to recover the captured ground.	yes
—do—	27/9/17	—	The following casualties were sustained during the action of yesterday and the subsequent shelling. Officers Killed - Lieut. E. J. LOWE. Officers wounded - Lieut. R.H. TURNER " R.E. INGRAM " H.C.W. CHAMBERS " G.H. GOULDBY " R.J. BROOKE " H. PARVIN " G. HOULDEN Missing - Capt. G.L. HILL (K) " C.N. NEWSUM (K) Lieut. P. GRANTHAM (K) OR estimates total casualties 350.	
—do—	—do—	6-30pm	During the day the enemy continued to shell our positions, especially in the neighbourhood of Hill 37 where the headquarters of this unit were situated at TULIP COTTAGES. A few casualties were incurred. The enemy for two hours shelled our positions very heavily with 5.9 of all calibres but principally 5.9. It is believed that a counter attack was made against the Brigade on our right but no attack developed against our own front. A patrol of 1 Officer & 12 men supplied by 36 R.F. to the 75th Lincoln Regiment. The expedition of gunnel can seen during our sight today was very slight. DOCHY FARM (D15c.10.15)	yes
		11.0pm	The Bn was relieved in the front line & moved to more or less.	yes

2449 Wt. W14957/M90 750,000 1/16 J.B.C. & A. Forms/C.2118/12.

Confidential

Army Form C. 2118.

WAR DIARY
or
INTELLIGENCE SUMMARY

(Erase heading not required.)

Place	Date	Hour	Summary of Events and Information	Remarks and references to Appendices
E.of Mue 37 (D.20 a)	27.9.17	—	A post of 1 NCO & 12 men at DOCHY FARM (D.15 c.10.15) handed over to 2/4 Leicesters. French running from D.14 d.8.1 to D.20 c.9.9 handed over to 2/4 Leicesters. A post of 1 Officer & 25 men at D.14 d.60.45 handed over to 2/5 Leicesters. French running from D.14 d.54 to D.14 d.70.15 handed over to 2/5 Leicesters. Battalion H.Q. in concrete blockhouse at D.20 a.65.70. The Battalion was in touch at time of relief with 2/4th Lincoln Regt on right and 2/5th Sherwood Foresters on left. On relief the Bn moved back to trenches W. of POMMERN CASTLE - D.19 a.2.2. Bn H.Q. was at BANK FARM.	
BANK FARM.	28.9.17		The day was quiet on the whole with little enemy shelling. An attempt was made to collect dead from front areas but only nine bodies were recovered. He found some of the Australian trenches were strewn with dead.	
—do—		10.30pm	The enemy commenced a bombardment of H.E. mixed with gas shells (mustard gas). There were no details and no respirators were worn. Subsequently the shells predominated and lachrymatory shells were also detected. The bombardment continued throughout the night but no move of any great intensity occurred. No shells dropping within 200' of the Battalion. No casualties were incurred.	
—do—	29.9.17		The day was quiet. The enemy shelled the reverse slopes of Hill 35 (D.19 b) from time to time but no shells fell near the Battalion. No casualties were incurred. The relief passed off	

2449 Wt. W14957/M90 750,000 1/16 J.B.C. & A. Forms/C.2118/12.

1/OTAGO REGT (New Zealand Forces).

Confidential

Army Form C. 2118.

WAR DIARY
or
INTELLIGENCE SUMMARY

(Erase heading not required.)

Instructions regarding War Diaries and Intelligence Summaries are contained in F. S. Regs., Part II. and the Staff Manual respectively. Title Pages will be prepared in manuscript.

Ref. to France: Belgium. Sheet: 27.y.28

Place	Date	Hour	Summary of Events and Information	Remarks and references to Appendices
BANK FARM (C.24.b) Sheet 28	29.9.17		Without incident. On relief the Bn. moved to DERBY CAMP (H.I.d. Central) Sheet 28) and was accommodated in tents. Enemy aircraft had previously dropped bombs on the camp but extent of damage was only two tents burning took place. 10 officers and 275 OR marches out of trenches. 21 officers 553 OR took same into the action of the 26th.	Apps
DERBY CAMP (H.I.d Central) Sheet 28	30.9.17	10.40 pm	The Bn. moved by train to TAY CAMP (L.15.b.4.b. Sheet 27) arriving 10.30 pm. Total casualties in action: Officers as noted in 27th Other Ranks Killed - 7 Died of wounds - 6 Missing - 74 Wounded - 193 " (at duty) - 7	Apps

W M Murphy
Lieut Colonel
Comdg 2/5 Lincoln Regt.

J. Hartfield
3.10.17

SECRET.

Copy No. 4

177th Infantry Brigade.

OPERATION ORDER No. 50.

Ref. GRAVENSTAFEL map attached.   24th September 1917.

1. Fifth Corps is resuming the attack on a date which has been communicated to Os.C. units.
   3rd Division will attack on the right, 59th Division on left.
   175th Inf.Bde. (58th Div.) will be on left of 59th Division; 8th Inf.Bde. (3rd Div.) (Headquarters C.30.a.95.15) will be on right of 59th Division.

2. The 59th Division will attack with two Brigades, the 177th on the right and the 178th on the left. Each brigade will attack with two battalions in the front line.
   The 176th Brigade will send one battalion to each of the 177th and 178th Inf.Bdes. The remaining two battalions of the 176th Brigade will be in Divisional reserve in the old British front line.

3. The attached map shows (1) inter-Divisional and Brigade and Battalion boundaries, (2) certain infantry halting places, (3) strong points to be constructed.
   It is of special importance to capture DOCHY FARM and the spur to the N.W. This ground once gained is to be retained at all costs.

4. The attack will be immediately preceded by a bombardment lasting two hours.

5. (a). The attack will be supported by the Field Artillery of 4 Divisions and 8 Army Brigades; also by 38 Siege and Heavy Batteries.

   (b). The Field Artillery barrage, which will consist of H.E. percussion and smoke shell, will move as follows:-
   Open 150 yards from forming up line and lift at 0 plus 3 minutes.
   Thence for 200 yards at rate of 100 yards in 4 minutes.
   Thence to RED Line at rate of 100 yards in 6 minutes.
   Thence to final objectives at rate of 100 yards in 8 minutes.
   All lifts will be 50 yards.

   (c). Barrage maps attached.

6. The D.M.G.O. is arranging for a Machine Gun barrage from 40 machine guns. This barrage will at first be on hostile strong points such as VAN ISACKERE Farm, DOCHY Farm, FOKKER Farm, TORONTO, OTTO Farm and will lift from those points just before the artillery barrage. It will then fire on the HANABEEK Valley and will subsequently lift to a general line BOURDEAUX Farm - BOETHOEK - GRAVENSTAFEL X roads.
   In addition arrangements will be made for a S.O.S. barrage in front of the final objective.
   The 177th and 178th Brigades will each have at their disposal 3 sections of their machine gun company.

7. Plan of attack will be as follows (each battalion attacking on a two-company frontage).

(a). At zero hour 2/4 LEICESTERS on right and 2/5 LEICESTERS on left will advance from position of assembly and gain the RED line.
Under the pause of the advance of the barrage they will reorganise and consolidate, occupying any captured strong points.

(b). At zero plus 100 minutes 2/4 LINCOLNS on right and 2/5 LINCOLNS on left will pass through the battalions in front, and, following the barrage, will gain the BLUE line.
Under cover of the final protective barrage they will reorganise and consolidate, occupying any captured strong points.

(c). On capture of final objective 2/4 LINCOLNS will detail troops to help in the capture of ISRAEL HOUSE and JACOB'S HOUSE, if not already taken by 8th Brigade.

8. 177th Machine Gun Coy.
1 Section will be attached to each of the LINCOLN Battalions.
2 guns will be attached to each of the LEICESTER Battalions.
In each case, after capture of objectives, these guns will be used in consolidation.

9. T.M. Battery.
2 guns will be attached to 2/4 LEICESTERS and 2 guns to 2/5 LEICESTERS for the purpose of bombarding TULIP COTTAGES and pill-box on HILL 37.

10. Positions of Headquarters and forming up places are as under:-
Headquarters.
    Brigade.   WIELTJE.

    Bde.Battle H.Qrs. BANK FARM.

    2/4 LINCOLNS.   IRMA, moving, on capture of 1st objective, to two Northern dugouts at D.20.b.4.6.

    2/5 LINCOLNS.   IBERIAN, moving, on capture of 1st objective, to TULIP COTTAGES.

    2/4 LEICESTERS }
    2/5 LEICESTERS }   Not yet settled.

    Reserve Battn.   POMMERN CASTLE, moving, on capture of
    (176th Bde.)   1st objective, to Southern dugout at D.20.b.4.6.

Forming-up Places.
    4th & 5th LEICESTERS. As close as possible to front line.

    4th & 5th LINCOLNS.   On the line - D.20.a.0.8. - Z. in ZEVENKOTE.

    Reserve Battn.   400 yards East of POMMERN CASTLE.
    (176th Bde.)

- 3 -

11. The Reserve Battalion will follow the 2/4 LINCOLNS at a distance of about 500 yards to a position about D.20.b.central to D.21.a.0.4.

12. In addition to the strong points shown on map already issued, the following will be made into strong points:-
   The three dugouts at D.21.a.7.9;
   The two dugouts at Western edge of DOCHY FARM, D.15.c.1.1.
   Os.C. 4th & 5th LINCOLNS will each be responsible for the construction and garrison of the two strong points in their area.
   1 Section R.E. Company will be attached to each of the LINCOLN Battalions to aid in the construction of these strong points.
   Garrison of each strong point: 2 Machine guns, and two Sections Infantry.

13. Definite units will be told off to capture known hostile strong points (such as TULIP COTTAGES, THE SNAG, LILAC COTTAGES, CABBAGE COTTAGES, PRIMROSE COTTAGES, Dugouts at D.20.b.4.6, VAN ISACKERE Farm, Dugouts at D.14.d.4.3, D.14.d.0.4. and D.14.d.7.6, DOCHY FARM, Dugouts at D.15.c.2.8, D.15.c.5.2, D.15.c.0.4. and D.15.c.7.0.).
   A garrison will be previously detailed for each of these strong points.

14. Battalions will provide their own carrying parties.

15. The 21st Squadron R.F.C. will detail a contact machine to be over the objective at about
   Zero plus 1 hour.
   Zero plus 1½ hours.
   Zero plus 2½ hours.
   and subsequently as ordered.
   xInfantry will light RED flares when called for by Klaxon horn or lights.
   xThe usual "counter-attack aeroplane" will be continuously in the air throughout the day from zero plus one hour till dusk.

16. Each battalion will repulse by immediate attack any hostile counter-attacks which may penetrate our line.

17. The 177th and 178th Brigades will form up for the attack by means of platoon pickets, tapes and protected lamps.

18. Tank orders.
   4 Tanks will co-operate on the 177th Brigade front.
   They will cross the front line at zero plus 10 minutes.
   Objectives:-
      2 tanks move via SNAG - PRIMROSE COTTAGES - ISACKERE FARM to dugouts at D.21.a.7.9.
      2 tanks via LILAC COTTAGES - DOCHY FARM to 5 dugouts onto D.15.c.4.0.
   On capture of final objective all four tanks will patrol up and down in front whilst consolidation is taking place.
   O.C. Tanks will be at IBERIAN FARM.

- 4 -

19. An officer from each unit will be at Brigade Headquarters at 6.30 p.m. and again at 8.30 p.m. 25th September, to synchronise watches.

20. Advanced Brigade Headquarters will open at zero hour.

21. Each battalion will arrange to get into touch with the troops on either flank at all the long pauses in the barrage.

22. Os.C. Battalions and Coys. on flanks of the Division will as far as possible meet before zero day the corresponding officers on their flanks so that operations can be discussed.
   8th EAST YORKS. take 1st objective.
   7th K.S.L.I. take 2nd objective.
   Both Headquarters at BORRY FARM.

23. Troops will be in position of assembly by 4 a.m. Z day.

24. All officers detailed for liaison duties will report at Brigade Headquarters at 4 p.m. 25th September.

25. Zero hour will be notified later.

26. Acknowledge.

Brigade Major, Major,
177th Infantry Brigade.

Issued at   by Special D.R.
Copy No. 1 - 59th Division.
        2 - 59th Division.
        3 - 4th Lincolns.
        4 - 5th Lincolns.
        5 - 4th Leicesters.
        6 - 5th Leicesters.
        7 - 177 M.G.Coy.
        8 - 177 Lt.T.M.Batty.
        9 - 176th Inf. Bde.
       10 - 178th Inf. Bde.
       11 - 8th Inf.Bde. (3rd Div.)
       12 - 5th S.Staffs.Regt.
       13 - Lt.Col.German, 5th Leicesters.
       14 - Tank Officer.
       15 - G.O.C.
       16 - Staff Captain.
       17 - Signalling Offr.
       18 - File.
       19 - War Diary.
       20 - War Diary.

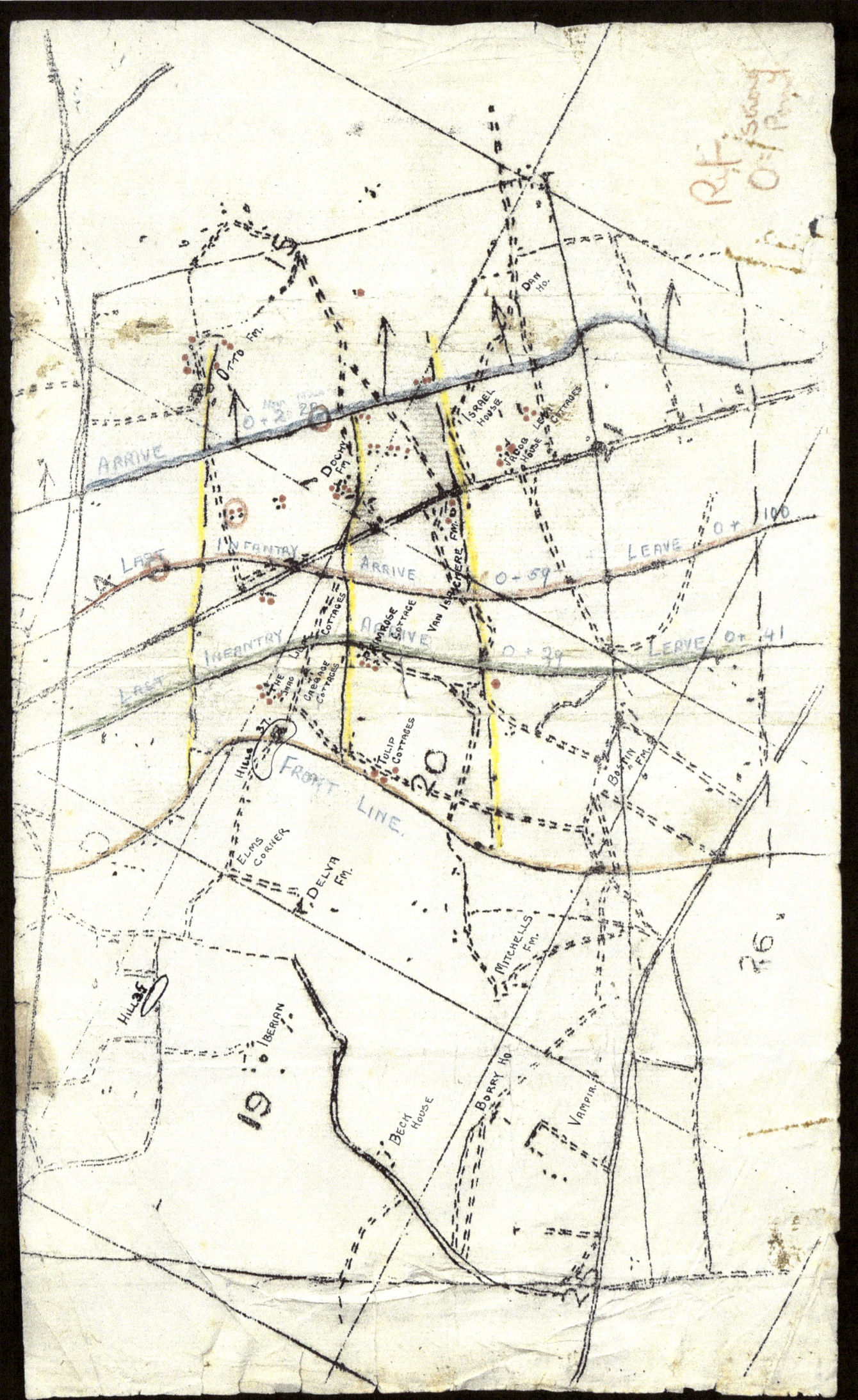

Account of the action by the 2/5th Bn. Lincolnshire Regiment on 26th September 1917.   Ref to Sheet 28.N.W & N.E. and special maps attached.

25.9.17

The original British front line was as shewn on barrage map attached to Brigade orders attached hereto.

The Battalion moved up from the trenches S. of WIELTJE at 11.0 pm moving by track 5 in single file, and formed up in the position of assembly, with the front along the line D.20.a.0.8 - 2 in ZEVENCOTE, with the right resting 50 yards S.E of DELVA FARM (D.20.a.0.3) the line extending for 400x. The forming up was carried out on tapes previously laid out, the limits of each platoon being marked out by pegs bearing the number of the platoon. The formation was as shewn on diagram attached.

The heavy bombardment of the enemy's position was short, from Zero minus 2 hours to Zero. The barrage was put down 150x in front of the original front line at Zero, 5.50 am. The troops moved in the formation in which they formed up and followed the 2/5 Leicester Regt who were in front. The 2/4th LINCOLNS were on our right and the 2/5th SHERWOOD FORESTERS on our left. The Battalion attacked on a two company frontage, B Coy (2Lieut H.C.W. CHAMBERS 3rd ESSEX Regt) being on the right and D Coy (Capt. G.L HILL) on the left. C Coy (Capt C.N. NEWSUM) was in support and A Coy (2Lieut W. PARVIN) in reserve & furnishing carrying parties. Only 20 officers took part in the attack, the remainder remaining at the Transport lines.

The formation shewn was maintained until the objectives were reached. The objectives were as stated in the operation order issued attached hereto. D Coy on the left met with practically no resistance, the concrete blockhouses at D.14.d.7.6 being non existent. D company commenced to dig a strong post at D.14.d.7.6 and sent a platoon across to assist B company in the capture of DOCHY FARM D.20.c.2.2. The remainder of the company commenced consolidation of the position behind the strong post.

B. Coy attacking DOCHY FARM as final objective were met by enemy m.g. and rifle fire but worked to the flanks of the blockhouses when the garrisons surrendered. Some 50 prisoners were captured here. The final consolidation was as shewn on the map. A Lewis Gun post was pushed forward in front of each company's position.

Dispositions at 8.30 a.m.

Strong Posts under construction at DOCHY FARM and at D 14 d. 7. 6.

Shell holes connected and deepened in rear of these posts for remainder of assaulting companies (B & D Coys).

The Support company consolidated a line of shell holes running approximately from D.14 d 5 4 to D 20. c 9 9.

The reserve company was used up for carrying parties and for runners.

The enemy's barrage was fairly heavy but the attack had pressed well on by the time it fell on our old front lines and the places of assembly, and did not cause many casualties. Finally it was directed against the newly taken positions when casualties were rather more. In particular the captured concrete blockhouses came in for more than usual attention and seem to be places to avoid.

The consolidation proceeded during the morning and afternoon. Late in the afternoon the enemy shelling increased very much in intensity and a small number of enemy were seen moving in front of our positions. A few men – of what regiments it is not known – commenced to retire as did the left Brigade of the 3rd Division on our right and a general retirement appeared imminent. Our own barrage fell in front of our positions and the returning troops were rallied and resumed their positions. The front line posts did not withdraw. The cause of this withdrawal has not been discovered but there was no heavy counter attack nor did any of the enemy attempt to pass through our barrage on this unit's front. By 8.30 p.m. all original positions were occupied.

The men behaved with the greatest gallantry

throughout and on several occasions had to be checked from passing through our own barrage to their objectives, especially during the wait behind the 2/5th Leicesters until zero plus 100 minutes when the battalion passed through the 5th Leicesters to our own objectives. It was found quite possible to keep up with the barrage which in the later stages moved 100x in 8 mins. The average distance from the barrage was about 50x.

Company commanders maintained the direction of the attack by means of compass bearings and these were very necessary as the country was almost unrecognisable. Our correct objectives were reached and the barrage closely followed the whole time.

The formation adopted was quite satisfactory and was maintained the whole way. The line of skirmishers was at times very irregular and difficult to maintain but it was found that the sections in file kept fairly well together and moved well. The lines were not deployed until our objectives were reached.

The enemy did not show much fight and the sections of A Coy attached to B and D coys as moppers up did not have much to do. Difficulty was experienced in thinning out the troops on the newly captured positions owing to the short distance between our final objective and the objective of the 2/5 Leicesters behind us.

Communication was difficult both forward and to the rear. Telephone lines were laid in triplicate forward but broke down in every case. Situation reports were sent back to Division by pigeon and reached their destination safely. Communication with Brigade was chiefly carried out through relays of runners as the telephones continually broke down. It would appear to be of first importance to have plenty of well trained runners and to establish relay posts at intervals of 100x or less if possible.

J. Chapman
Capt. A/Lt. Col.
2/5th Bn Lincoln Regt

In the Field.
3.10.17.

Attack formation of 2/4th Lincolnshire Regt in the attack on German position on 26.9.17

D Company   B Company
<--------- 200ˣ ---------><----------- 200ˣ ----------->

<-- No.14 Plat   <-- No.13 Plat -->   <-- No.6 Plat   <-- No.5 Platoon -->   No.5 Plat
(1 Sect: extenders) (1 Sect: Palisades)   (Sect (Grenadiers) Extended) (Sect (Grenadiers) Extended)   with 1 Sect from A Coy as "Moppers up"

<-- No.15 Plat -->   <-- No.7 Plat -->
|| || || || || || || || || || || || || || || || || ||
|| || || || || || || || || || || || || || || || || ||

δ Coy H.Q.   δ Coy H.Q.

<-- No.10 Plat --   <-- C Company — 200ˣ -->   <-- No.9 Plat -->
|| || || || || || || || || || || || || || || || || ||
|| || || || || || || || || || || || || || || || || ||

<-- No.11 Plat -->
|| || || || || || || || || || || || || || || || || ||
|| || || || || || || || || || || || || || || || || ||

δ Coy H.Q.

<-- No.3 Plat -- >< -- 2 Sect No.2 Plat --> < -- 2 sect No.1 Plat -->
|| || || || || || || || || || || || || || || || || ||
|| || || || || || || || || || || || || || || || || ||

δ Coy H.Q.

Direction of Advance <----

Nos 13 & 14 Platoons each with 1 Section from A Coy as "moppers up"

Total Depth of forming up position 200ˣ

|| = Section moving in file.

1:10 000 K.3. EDITION I. Parts of { 28 N.E. / 28 N.W.

final objectives & line of consolidation. Strong posts.

FIELD SURVEY COY. R.E. (2591) 16-3-17 Scale. 1:10,000.

Confidential

Vol 9

War Diary of the 9/5th Battalion
The Lincolnshire Regiment

from 1/10/17
to 31/10/17

F.J. Garrison Major
Cmdg 9/5 Lincoln Rgt

confidential · ORIGINAL · Army Form C. 2118.

Map References to France and Belgium. HAZEBROUCK

OCTOBER 1917

WAR DIARY
or
INTELLIGENCE SUMMARY
(Erase heading not required.)

Instructions regarding War Diaries and Intelligence Summaries are contained in F.S. Regs., Part II. and the Staff Manual respectively. Title Pages will be prepared in manuscript.

Place	Date	Hour	Summary of Events and Information	Remarks and references to Appendices
POPERINGHE	1/10/17		Bn. accomodated at TA1 CAMP (L.15,c-4,6) in tents. (Sheet 27 Ed. 2 1/40,000) Strength of Battalion	ferry
do.	2/10/17		Bn. moved from TA1 CAMP to BAS HAMEL (G.5, 12-72.) HAZEBROUCK (5A) by Bus	ferry
BAS HAMEL	2/10/17 to 6/10/17		Bn accomodated in billets. Training carried out daily. Close order drill and preliminary instruction in individual subjects. Lewis Gun, Bombing, Rifle grenades, machine, snipers.	ferry
do.	6/10/17		Moves by bus and march route to LUGY (C.b. 05-28.) HAZEBROUCK 5A Accomodated in billets.	ferry
LUGY	6/10/17 to 10/10/17		Training continued as above.	ferry
-do-	10/10/17		Moves by march route to PRESSY-LES-PERNES. (E.1. 06. 68. LENS 11) Accomodates in billets. C.O. Adjutant, Intelligence Officer and Signalling Officer route 3rd Canadian Brigade in the new LENS.	ferry
PRESSY-LES-PERNES.	11/10/17		Moves by march route to DIVION (G.1. 03-75. LENS 11) Accomodates in billets.	ferry
DIVION	12/10/17		Moves by march route to PETIT SERVINS (H.2. 7-9. LENS 11) Accomodates in billets.	ferry
DIVION	13/10/17	9.0 am	Moved by march route to SOUCHEZ (I.2. 9-67. LENS 11)	ferry

Army Form C. 2118.

WAR DIARY
or
INTELLIGENCE SUMMARY
(Erase heading not required.)

Map Reference FRANCE. LENS. Sheets 36.c. S.W. 3 and S.W. 4

Place	Date	Hour	Summary of Events and Information	Remarks and references to Appendices
SOUCHEZ	13/10/17	5.15 p.m	The Battalion moves up to relieve the 16th Canadian Scottish in the front line, AVION SECTOR, in the front line. The relief passed off without incident.	
AVION	14/10/17	1.30 A.m	The Battalion dispositions were as follows (See map attached) Right Front line. Held by 'A' Coy. from N.33.d.5.3. to N.33.c.9.5 by a series of posts, evenly distributes along the frontage. Nineteen posts in all. Lewis Guns at N.33.d.5.3. N.33.c.9.4. N.33.c.4.5. By night these posts are kept by garrison of 1 NCO and 4 to 6 men. During the day they are withdrawn to AVION TRENCH (T.3.a.). Lewis Gun posts are not withdrawn. Coy. H.Q. T.3.a.6.5. (AVION TRENCH). Left Front Line. Held by 'C' Coy from N.33.c.4.5. to N.32.c.95.45. by a series of posts evenly distributed along the frontage - twelve posts in all. Lewis Gun posts at N.33.c.3.7. N.33.c.25.70. N.33.a.0.5.20. Stay the posts are withdrawn by day to AVION Trench (N.32.d.) returning at night. There is a Platoon accommodated by day in cellars at N.33.c.3.7. which by night holds 3 posts from N.33.c.45.60. N.33.c.25.80. Coy. H.Q. N.32.d. 65.40. (AVION Trench). Support Coy. Held by "B" Coy. AVION Trench from T.3.a.7.4. to N.35.d.75.10. The Coy is distributed in six supports along the trench. Bn. H.Q. T.3.a. 15.60. with no Lewis Gun.	✓

Army Form C. 2118.

WAR DIARY or INTELLIGENCE SUMMARY

Map Reference _____

(Erase heading not required.) FRANCE LENS Sheet 36c S.W.3 & 36c S.W.4 (10,000)

Instructions regarding War Diaries and Intelligence Summaries are contained in F. S. Regs., Part II. and the Staff Manual respectively. Title Pages will be prepared in manuscript.

Place	Date	Hour	Summary of Events and Information	Remarks and references to Appendices
AVION (N.33.) & N.32.	14/10/17		Dispositions (cont.) Reserve Coy. Accommodated in dugouts at T.2.b. 2.8. (BEAVER Tr.). Also Coy H.Q. with three Lewis Guns. The Support Coy. maintains two Anti Aircraft Lewis Guns in Avion Travel at T.2.b.9.7 and N.32.d.5.1. These are to deal with low flying enemy planes. Bn. H.Q. T.3.c.65.90 (SOUVES Road) Flanking Battalions. Right 29th Canadians. Left 4/5th LEICESTER REGT. Touch maintained with both flanks by patrols. There are 5 Vickers Guns and 6 Stokes Guns in the Bn. Area. The trenches are in fair condition. Some trenches rather muddy. Front line trenches within 400 x of front line but passable. No trenches revetted.	
- do -	- do -	8.0am to 7.30pm	Enemy's artillery fairly active, distributing shells (4.2" and 5.9") freely on our area. Our counter battery was sometimes. Own artillery replied effectively. Enemy's minenwerfer shelled own front line about 7.30 p.m. from the railway embankment in N.33.b and d but were quickly silenced by own artillery.	
- do -	15/10/17	12.30 am	Patrol found touch with two enemy posts at N.33.c.5.7. Enemy's entrenchments.	yes.
		6.0am to 8.0pm	Work done during night. Cleaning and repairing front line trenches, fire steps and parapets and clearing of CYRIL C.T. and AVION Tr. Enemy's activity limited to artillery which shelled own support trenches and C.T.s frequently. Our sentries 3 casualties (wounded). The enemy infantry shows	

WAR DIARY or INTELLIGENCE SUMMARY

Army Form C. 2118.

(Erase heading not required.) FRANCE. LENS Sheet 36c.S.W.3 y 36C.S.W.4

Map Reference. Scale 1/10000

Place	Date	Hour	Summary of Events and Information	Remarks and references to Appendices
AVION. (N32 & N33)	15.10.17	8.0pm	Rifle activity - does not occur. Snipe. His minenwerfers spared on our front line but were quickly silenced by our artillery in reqeust. Enemys aircraft have been active over our front line, and also our own. Work done during night - continuation of 14-15/10 - clearing & repairing front line. Support line (AVION) and C.T.S.	four
- do -	16.10.17		A normal day. Enemys artillery active as usual. Ours has replied vigorously.	four
- do -	17.10.17		Bn. was relieved in the front line trenches by the 2/4th LEICESTER RGT. Relief passes uneventfully. Bn on relief became right Support Battalion to Brigade and moved into dugouts in RED TRENCH. Relief completed 11.5pm. Dispositions :-	four
GIVENCHY (S.10.a & c.)	- do -		Bn. H.Q. and D & B Coys in large dugout in RED TRENCH. S.12.b.6.4. A Coy in dugouts in RED TRENCH S.12.a.5.6. C " " " " " T.7.a.4.4. In touch with 2/5 Leicester Rgt on left and 6th GLOUCESTER RGT (48th Divn.) on right.	four
GIVENCHY (S.10.a & c)	17.10.17 to 21.10.17		Continued in Support in RED TRENCH. Each night 200 men were found for working parties in forward area. By day working parts of 50 men were found for work in C.T.S.	four
	21.10.17		Bn. relieved in RED TRENCH by 2/7th Bn. SHERWOOD FORESTERS. Bn on relief moved to SOUCHEZ CAMP. SOUCHEZ. Going into Divisional Reserve.	four
SOUCHEZ (36C.S.W.)	22.10.17 to 29.10.17		Bn. remained at Souchez providing working parties for C's in forward area. & all about 2 x 3 men were 'employed' daily. Training of Lewis Gunners, Bombers, Snipers, Signallers etc. was continued when men available.	four

2449 Wt. W14957/Mgo 750,000 1/16 J.B.C. & A. Forms/C.2118/12.

Army Form C. 2118.

WAR DIARY
or
INTELLIGENCE SUMMARY
(Erase heading not required.)

Map Reference. FRANCE LENS Sheet 36 c.S.W.1. 1/10000

Place	Date	Hour	Summary of Events and Information	Remarks and references to Appendices
LENS.	29/01/17	11.5pm	Bn moved from SOUCHEZ and relieves 2/6th SOUTH STAFFORDSHIRE Regt in the front line trenches of the right subsector of 59th Division Left Sector. Relief passed off without event. The dispositions taken up by this Battalion were as follows:— Right Front Line Coy. (D Coy) holds the front line from N.20.C.00.40.1. to N.20.e.13.90. by a series of posts as under.	See Appendices

10.1. N.20.C.09.10. 1 N.C.O. 7 men
2. C. 05.20. (centre) 1 NCO 7 " — LEWIS GUN.
3. C. 06.23. (do) 1 NCO 5 "
4. C. 10.30. 1 NCO 7 " — Lewis Gun.
5. C. 09.35. 1st 2NCO 9 " — Post H.Q.
6. C. 10.50. (Rationing post supplies by No.5
7. C. 18.65. 1 NCO 4 men.
8. C. 20.70. 1 " 6 " — Lewis Gun.
9. C. 22.78. 1 " 4 "
10. C. 12.87. 1st 2 " 10 " — Lewis Gun and Platoon H.Q.

Coy H.Q. N.19.d.35.30. (cellar) 1 Officer. 14 O.R.

All posts are on the East side of LENS — ARRAS road except No.10 which is in ARGYLE TRENCH (W. Side of road).

In addition this company is supplied with a fighting patrol of 1 Officer and 14 OR with Lewis Gun from the Reserve Company. Patrol remains in situ throughout

Army Form C. 2118.

WAR DIARY
or
INTELLIGENCE SUMMARY
(Erase heading not required.) Map Ref. FRANCE - LENS. Sheet. 36c. S.W.1 1/10,000

Place	Date	Hour	Summary of Events and Information	Remarks and references to Appendices
LENS.	29.10.17	11.5pm	Left Front Line Coy (B Coy) holds the front line from N.20.c. 13.90 to N.29.a. 00.50. by a series of posts as under.	
			No.11. N.20.c. 14.92. 1 NCO. 4 men.	
			12. N.20.c. 10.97. 1 " 4 "	
			13. a. 10.06. 1 " 4 " Lewis Gun.	
			14. a. 10.12. 1 " 4 "	
			15. 08.16. 1 " 4 "	
			16. 17.24. 1 " 4 "	
			17. 15.35. 1 " 4 "	
			18. 23.33. 1 " 4 " Lewis Gun.	
			19. 05.36. 1 " 4 " do.	
			20. 00.50. 1 " 4 "	
			Coy HQ. N.19.d. 38.80. 3 Off. 3 NCOs. 14 men. 1 Lewis Gun.	
			This company is supplied with a fighting patrol of 1 Officer and 14 OR with a Lewis Gun, by the support company. The patrol remains out all night.	
			Support Company. 2 Off. 65. OR.	
			1 Platoon with Lewis Gun at N.25.a. 75.25. Lewis Gun by night in posts at N.25.b. 30.50.	
			1 Platoon with 2 Lewis Guns at N.19.c. 97. This platoon furnishes fighting patrol for left front company.	
			Coy HQ. N.30.a. 54 with one Lewis Gun.	

Army Form C. 2118.

WAR DIARY
or
INTELLIGENCE SUMMARY
(Erase heading not required.)

Map Ref. FRANCE. LENS. Sheet 36.c.SW.1 1/10000

Instructions regarding War Diaries and Intelligence Summaries are contained in F. S. Regs., Part II. and the Staff Manual respectively. Title Pages will be prepared in manuscript.

Place	Date	Hour	Summary of Events and Information	Remarks and references to Appendices
LENS.	29.10.17	11.55pm	Reserve Company. 4 Off. 74 O.R. Coy H.Q. and Coy unit 3 Lewis guns at M.30.a.85.30. This company furnishes fifteen patrol for night front company. Bn. H.Q. M.30.a.4.5. 6 Off. 45 O.R. Band maintained unit 2/5 LEICESTER REGT on left. 2/6th SHERWOOD FORESTERS on right. Observation Post M.14.c.45.50. (rear) N.19.d.7D.50. (forward).	
- do -	30.10.17		Enemy quiet the whole day. Movement observed in back area.	
- do -	31.10.17	6.0am	A party of 6 enemy crawled up to our post at N.20.e.14.9.2. and threw a kind of incendiary (?) bomb on to the post. Flames and thick smoke were produced. One enemy was wounded by own fire but he got away. Under cover of smoke. The post appeared contain a suitable substance with a disturbing and severe action. We suffered no casualties.	
		6.0pm	Day uneventful. We discharged gas clouds from our lines on 6 selected enemy positions. No retaliation was offered.	
		12.R. midnight	From 8-11.0 pm and at 10.45 pm we directed bursts of heavy artillery fire in approach to German line on 6 relief zones suspected.	

2449 Wt. W14957/M90 750,000 1/16 J.B.C. & A. Forms/C.2118/12.

Army Form C. 2118.

WAR DIARY
or
INTELLIGENCE SUMMARY
(Erase heading not required.)

Place	Date	Hour	Summary of Events and Information	Remarks and references to Appendices
LENS	31/10/17	—	Following Officers have joined during the month	
			Major F.D. Harrison 3rd Leicesters 14.10.17	
			" J.C. Lyon 9/6. N. Staffords. 23.10.17	
			2/Lieut. W.A. Ball 3rd Lincolns 24.10.17	
			" A.J. Healey " "	
			" W.E.C. Jones " "	
			" P.C. Renshaw " 25.10.17	
			" L.G. Moss " 24.10.17	
			" J. Wyer " "	
			" L.W. Hawkins " "	
			" J.C. Myers " x25.10.17	
			" M.A. Norton " 31.10.17	
			" F. Sharpe " "	

J. McGuley
31/10/17

F.D. Harrison Lt. Major
Comdg 2/5 Lincoln Rgt

Confidential.

War Diary of the 2/5th Battalion
The Lincolnshire Regiment
from
1st to 30th November, 1917

1/12/17

M.W.H.H.
Lieut. Colonel
Cmdg 2/5th Lincolnshire Regt.

CONFIDENTIAL ORIGINAL

Army Form C. 2118.

2/5 LINCOLN REGT **WAR DIARY** or **INTELLIGENCE SUMMARY**

Map Ref. FRANCE. LENS. Sheet 36c S.W.1. 1/10,000.

NOVR. 1917

(Erase heading not required.)

Place	Date	Hour	Summary of Events and Information	Remarks and references to Appendices
LENS.	1/11/17 to 6/11/17	—	The Bn. remained in the LENS sector during the period, maintaining the same dispositions. On the night 2/3 November an inter-company relief took place the same distribution of Coys being maintained. Right front line C coy. Left front line A coy. Support Coy D coy. Reserve Coy B. The enemy showed no great activity of any kind. He was inclined to work about in front of our line but a few days pumping in which we obtained 9 hits have taught caution. A few nights fusiliers were sent over by machines to our front line and these 65 traps and 5 casualties were sustained. The importance of constant watching and our artillery has been very active shelling enemy position and tall gas shell cannot be over-emphasised. The enemy's activity has been very active shelling enemy position and tall areas. The trenches are not good but are being rapidly improved. A good deal of work was done on the front line deepening and traversing & the man C.T. has been deepened and duckboarded a considerable length.	
	6/11/17	—	The Bn. was relieved by the 1/4 LEICESTER RGT. On relief the Bn. moved into CITÉ de ROLLENCOURT (M.27.b) where it was in Bde Reserve.	
CITÉ de ROLLENCOURT	7/11/17 to 13/11/17	—	In Bde reserve. Working parties were furnished by day and night to work on communication trenches in forward area. No artillery activity was shown by the enemy as regards the area occupied by the battalion. Few men were evidenced whilst on working parties.	
	13/11/17	7.30 p.m.	Battalion relieved by 3rd Alexandria Battalion entrained at RED MILL SIDING and proceeded to SERVINS via SERVINS aux H.Q. A and B Coys billeted in GRAND SERVINS and C & D.	

Army Form C. 2118.

WAR DIARY
or
INTELLIGENCE SUMMARY

(Erase heading not required.)

Map Ref FRANCE Sheet- 36 B, 51 e, 57 c
1/40,000

Place	Date	Hour	Summary of Events and Information	Remarks and references to Appendices
GRAND SERVINS	13/11/17		2nd D Coys. billeted in PETIT SERVINS.	6 GB
	14/11/17		No training took place, the day being devoted to cleaning equipment &c.	8 GB
	15/11/17		Bn. carried out Advanced Guards practice by half-battalions.	8 GB
	16/11/17		Bn. carried out Advanced Guard practice by Companies & Company arrangements.	8 GB
	17/11/17	Noon	Battalion proceeded by march route to WANQUETIN, where the Battalion was accommodated in huts at K 32 c. 9.5. 9 men fell out, but 6 of these rejoined their respective Coys., the remaining 3 being brought along by Horse Ambulance. Weather was fine.	6 GB
WANQUETIN	18/11/17		Church parade for non-conformists Corps. and specialist Officers carried out. A stock taking of stores and equipment.	8 GB
	19/11/17		Officers and N.C.O's practised rapid reconnaissances and quick appreciation of various situations.	6 GB
BELLACOURT	20/11/17	4 pm.	Bn. moved by march route to BELLACOURT, Accommodation in billets. H.Q's at the CHATEAU at R 31 a. 8. 0.	6 GB
	21/11/17	11 pm.	Bn. under Warning Orders first to call to march to ACHIET AREA and afterwards to entrain BEDFORD	6 GB
	22/11/17		Bn. moved by march route to ACHIET LE PETIT where it was accommodated in BEDFORD CAMP.	8 GB
ACHIET-LE-PETIT	23/11/17	5 am.	Orders received that Bn. would entrain for ETRICOURT or FINS.	8 GB
DESSART WOOD	24/11/17		Bn. moved by march route to ACHIET-LE-GRAND where it entrained for FINS. Arrived at FINS at 12.30 pm and proceeded to DESSART WOOD. Bn. accommodated in Tents.	8 GB
	25/11/17		Bn. occupied in cleaning up the camp.	8 GB
	26/11/17	9 - 11.30	Church Parade for C. of E., Nonconformists and Roman Catholics. Specialist training carried out in all branches of specialist training.	8 GB
	27/11/17	9 12.30	Specialist training carried out in the Tents.	8 GB
TRESCAULT			Bn. proceeded by march route to TRESCAULT being accommodated in huts and bivouacs to the No 12 & HAVRINCOURT WOOD.	8 GB

2449 Wt. W14957/M90 750,000 1/16 J.B.C. & A. Forms/C.2118/12.

Army Form C. 2118.

WAR DIARY
or
INTELLIGENCE SUMMARY

(Erase heading not required.)

Map Ref FRANCE. Sheet 57^c 1/140,000

Place	Date	Hour	Summary of Events and Information	Remarks and references to Appendices
TRESCAULT	28/11/17	1.45pm	Bn. proceeded by march route to FLESQUIERES. The Battalion was accommodated in the HINDENBURG SUPPORT LINE S.W. of FLESQUIERES, Bn. H.Q. being established in a dug out at K.21.a. 15.50. Enemy artillery fired about 12 rounds round about Bn. H.Q. No casualties were sustained.	E.S.R.
FLESQUIERES	29/11/17		Enemy artillery between 11.0 and 12.0 o'clock in the morning again fired several shots into Keneles obtaining one direct hit on a shelter, killing and wounding 7 Officers:- Killed - Capt. C.D.R. Jacobs, 3rd Devon Regt., attchd 7/5 Lincoln Regt. Wounded - Capt. Y.A. Richardson 2/Lieuts. F.C. STEWART (4th Norfolk Regt.), S. PLOWMAN, K.A.S. FOWLER, L. MASON, L.W.H. HAWKINS, and M.A. NORTON. That of Rose wounds were slight.	868
	30/11/17	Noon	Bn. received orders to dig trenches to the N.W. and W. of FLESQUIERES for the purpose of defending this village should the enemy break through. Dispositions of Coys. A Coy. K.18.c.5.8. to K.17.a.9.7. B Coy K.17.a.7.5 to K.23.b.5.9, C. Coy. K.23.b.5.9. to K.23.b.8.5. Trenches were dug and a Rifle wire entanglement placed and in position before midnight. D Coy. was Coy. in reserve and remained in HINDENBURG SUPPORT LINE close to Bn. H.Q.	E.S.R.

[signature]
Lieut. Colonel
Cmdg 7/5 Lincolnshire Regt.

Confidential

War Diary of the 2/5th Bn. The
Lincolnshire Regiment
from
to 31/10/17

1/10/17

M.S.W.???
Lieut Colonel
Cmdg 2/5th Lincoln Regt.

Army Form C. 2118.

WAR DIARY
or
INTELLIGENCE SUMMARY
(Erase heading not required.)

Ref. France Sheet 57c. N.E. 20000.

Place	Date	Hour	Summary of Events and Information	Remarks and references to Appendices
FLESQUIERES	1.12.17	—	Strength 9 Officers 355 OR. Bn disposed as for 30.11.17 in the vicinity of FLESQUIERES. Bn continued at night on the trenches commenced on 30.11.17 for the defence of the village. Trenches are now 3 to 4' deep and some wire has been erected.	fire
— do —	2.12.17	—	Bn went into the line near BOURLON WOOD relieving 2/5th N. STAFFORD Regt. Disposition as follows.	fire
BOURLON WOOD	3.12.17	1·0 am	The Bn held the front line from gap with 3 companies, from F.14 d. 1.3 to F.20 d. 9.4. The line was held by a series of posts. There being no continuous trench. A Coy with right with 9 posts. B Coy centre with 7 posts. C Coy left with 5 posts. Posts were alternately Lewis gun and riflemen posts. D. Coy was in support & were accommodated in dugouts about F.26 b.2.5. B.H.Q. and R.A.P. dugouts F.20 b.5.3. Bn maintained with the 2/5th Leicester Rgt on the right and the 2/4th Lincoln Rgt on the left. There appears to be no well defined enemy line opposite. The Germans to be holding elements of trench in F.14 d. and F.20, a but the line of posts run small copse in F.21 a. was not held by them. Bn line of posts ran about 100ˣ W of the copse.	
BOURLON WOOD	3.12.17		Dispositions unchanged. The 2/4 LEICESTERS on our left were relieved by the 2/4 LINCOLN RGT. The enemy's activity has been confined to artillery work. The front line was very shelled intermittently during the day + also HQ. A number of gas shells (phosgene gas) were fired into the valley about F.20 a.1.1. The wind being from the Gas down to Bn HQ where box respirators were worn for an hour. There were no casualties.	

Army Form C. 2118.

WAR DIARY
or
INTELLIGENCE SUMMARY
(Erase heading not required.)

Ref France Sheet 57c N.E.

Place	Date	Hour	Summary of Events and Information	Remarks and references to Appendices
BOURLON WOOD	3.12.17		Enemy M.G. fired at intervals throughout the night. We suffered 2 casualties.	
- do -	4.12.17		Enemy activity again confined to artillery fire. In order to reduce the salient of which our line formed a part, a withdrawal was carried out to the FLESQUIERES LINE. Pack forms and limbers were brought up and ammunition and stores were removed before the withdrawal commenced. The withdrawal was made from the left by Platoons. One Platoon remained behind in the Coy's Company frontage to cover the withdrawal. The first company commenced the withdrawal about 9.45pm and at intervals in four's per Platoon. Platoons more independently across country to FLESQUIERES and took up their allotted position in the Flesquieres line. The enemy seemed totally unaware of the withdrawal. There were no fire from his artillery beyond the ordinary routine hung of the night. The withdrawal was concluded in good order, without casualty, and dispositions taken up at Flesquieres as follows. The existing trenches N and N.N.1 Flesquieres between the limits K.17.c.2.2. and K.17.d.7.6. were held by A and B Coys with C and D Coys in support on the Hindenburg support line about K.24.a.1.6. Bn. H.Q. in dugout K.24.a.1.6.	
FLESQUIERES	5.12.17		No signs of the enemy following up were observed until about 3.0pm when motor lorries were seen in FONTAINE-notre DAME and small bodies of enemy men seen in neighbourhood of BOURLON WOOD. Our front was still covered by a rearguard consisting of the 9/17th SHERWOOD FORESTERS but two companies 1/4 & Lincolns. at night line commenced digging	

Army Form C. 2118.

WAR DIARY
or
INTELLIGENCE SUMMARY

(Erase heading not required.)

Ref. FRANCE Sheet 57C NE. 20000

Instructions regarding War Diaries and Intelligence Summaries are contained in F.S. Regs, Part II. and the Staff Manual respectively. Title Pages will be prepared in manuscript.

Place	Date	Hour	Summary of Events and Information	Remarks and references to Appendices
FLESQUIERES	5.12.17	—	A new front line trench running from K.15.a.7.0.45 to K.17.b.3.5. thus bringing the front line up to the advanced posts of the 1/5 London Regt. on our left. A the right we were the 2/5 LEICESTER Regt. This new front line trench was dug to 3'6" and occupied by seven Lewis Gun posts. During the digging the enemy shelled continuously inflicting about a dozen casualties. Capt H.V. NEWSUM was sent down suffering from Shell Gas.	Jw
— do —	6.12.17	3.0 pm	Our outpost line fell back on our front line trench & an enemy attack developed. The brunt of the attack fell on the 2/5th Leicesters Regt on our right and no enemy came up against our trenches although we were able to bring fire to bear against the advancing German's the right battalion. Enemy shelling two heavy and we sustained some twenty casualties. Patrols were sent out to Battalion on right and Left to keep in touch. Communication difficult owing to enemy shelling.	
		8.0 pm	Work was continued on the new front line commenced last night and a new C.T. commenced from K.15.a.3.5 to K.15.c.2.5. This trench was dug 3 feet wide and 3'6" deep. During the night fighting patrols were sent out during the night to prevent the enemy reconnoitering our line and to prevent him	

WAR DIARY
or
INTELLIGENCE SUMMARY. Maps Ref

(Erase heading not required.)

Army Form C. 2118.

FRANCE Sheet 57c NE

Hour, Date, Place	Summary of Events and Information	Remarks and References to Appendices
FLESQUIERES 6/12/17	(cont⁰) from digging in near our line. Harassing fire by artillery and machine guns was arranged during the night to prevent the enemy digging.	
7/12/17 — do —	2/Lieut. E. GARRAD just obtain intelligence from officers of Skele Res. No signs of connected enemy trenches seen but since posts has been dug some 500ˣ in front of our position. Enemy shelling continued throughout the day and we suffered some casualties. The same patrol and harassing fire was carried on during the night and work in trenches continued. Dispositions now were — Right front line. A Coy. K.13 a 7.4 to K.18 a w.5 Left " " B " K.18 c 4.5 to K.17 b 9.5. Right Support Coy C. accommodated in dugouts K.18 a 7.2 Left " " D " " " " K.17 d 9.6 Bn H.Q. Dugout K.13 c. 7.4. Unit on right flank 2/5 Leicesters " " left " 1/6 London Rgt.	Jeu
8/12/17 to 9/12/17 — do —	Enemy continues digging posts in front of our position but shows no activity other than with his artillery and occasional machine gun fire. Patrols were sent out nightly to keep away enemy patrols and to establish German line. Our casualties during these two nights were slight.	
9/12/17 11·0 pm — do —	By 2/6 Bn Sherwood Foresters in relief. Battalion moves to TRESCAULT.	

Army Form C. 2118.

WAR DIARY
or
INTELLIGENCE SUMMARY.
(Erase heading not required.)   Ref. FRANCE Sheet. 57 c 1/40000

Instructions regarding War Diaries and Intelligence Summaries are contained in F.S. Regs., Part II. and the Staff Manual respectively. Title pages will be prepared in manuscript.

Hour, Date, Place	Summary of Events and Information	Remarks and References to Appendices
10/12/17 TRESCAULT	The Bn was accommodated in shelters on the OLD British Front Line. Enemy planes were active at 7.0 a.m. firing MG. Machine guns and dropping bombs.	
do 12.30pm – do –	Bn moved by march route to LECHELLE, accommodated in huts in P.25.b.	JCy
11/12/17 to 13/12/17 LECHELLE	Men were bathed and then clothing changed. Training was carried out on 12/13 Dec during the morning. – Bayonet fighting, Drill and Instructional instruction in Specialist, Lewis Gun, Bombing.	JCy JCy
13/12/17 14/12/17 to 17/12/17 TRESCAULT MAVRINCOURT	Bn moves to TRESCAULT. Accommodated on 10/12/17 Bn moved to the British Front Line in R.32. Accommodated in trenches, tents and shelters. Working parties were furnished each day for work under R.E Supervision on CTs and Hindenburg Line.	JCy
17/12/17 4.30pm FLESQUIERES	Bn moved into left support in FLESQUIERES Sector - relieving the 9/16th SHERWOOD FORESTERS. Bn was disposed in HINDENBURG SUPPT LINE as follows. Coys disposed equally from right to left along trench from R.24.a.5.4 to R.17.d.6.1. in order B.C.A.D. Bn HQ. K.24.a.25.45.	JCy

Army Form C. 2118.

WAR DIARY
or
INTELLIGENCE SUMMARY.

(Erase heading not required.) Ref FRANCE 57°.NE. 20000.

Instructions regarding War Diaries and Intelligence Summaries are contained in F.S. Regs., Part II. and the Staff Manual respectively. Title pages will be prepared in manuscript.

Hour, Date, Place		Summary of Events and Information	Remarks and References to Appendices
17.12.17 to 22.12.17	FLESQUIERES	Bn continued in Support line. Working parties supplied day and night for Tunnelling Corps making dugouts in the Support line. Working parties were furnished for R.E. to dig C.T.s. back from front line to Support line. Rear was done shelling by the enemy. Lieut H.W. WRIGHT and 6 other ranks were wounded. Lieut F.B. SMITH joined for duty.	
23.12.17	— do —	Bn was relieved in Flesquieres Support by 3/4th Royal West Kent Regt and moved to rest to our British short line M.C. 32.	
23.12.17 24.12.17 25.12.17	ROCQUINY — do —	Bn moved to huts at ROCQUINY. Cleaning equipment. Bn moved to TINQUES. Bn moved off at 5.20 am. to RAPAUME where it entrained for TINQUES. Marched from TINQUES to AMBRINES where accommodated in billets. Transport moved by road except Rations, Lewis gun wagons, mess cart and machine cart.	
26.12.17 to 31.12.17	AMBRINES	Bn carried out training. Drill and Bayonet fighting every day. Preliminary instruction in Lewis gun, bombing, signalling, scouting.	

Cmdg 1/5 London Regt

Army Form C. 2118.

WAR DIARY
or
INTELLIGENCE SUMMARY.
(Erase heading not required.)

CONFIDENTIAL

WAR DIARY
of
2/5th Bn. Lincolnshire Regt.
from
1/1/18 to 31/1/18

Tebyr Major
Cmdg 2/5th Lincolnshire Regt.

1/2/18

Army Form C. 2118.

WAR DIARY
or
INTELLIGENCE SUMMARY
(Erase heading not required.)

Ref. France Sheet 51 c / 40000.

Hour, Date, Place	Summary of Events and Information	Remarks and References to Appendices
1/1/18 to 31/1/18 AMBRINES (I.3)	Battalion in billets. Training carried out daily. Close order drill was carried out each day to smarten and steady the men. Bayonet fighting and Recreational training were specialised in throughout the latter portion being and running were to the chief feature. During the month a Brigade run was held in which every available man ran. The battalion finished second with 47 men in. Time allowed 1 hour. Distance 9 miles. Platoon and company training was carried out in open warfare attack, movements in artillery formation, attack against strong points. Numbery received special attention, each man fires a course of 25 rounds on the 30" range and a 2nd course of 50 rounds on 300' range. Individual training, Lewis Gunners, Bombers, Rifle Grenadiers, stretcher bearers, runners, scouts & snipers was also carried out. During the month the health of the men has considerably improved and (Regent Baths & changing of clothes) have resulted in most of them being free from body lice. Blankets have been stored and the men ordered clothing Regimental	

Army Form C. 2118.

WAR DIARY
or
INTELLIGENCE SUMMARY.
(Erase heading not required.)

Instructions regarding War Diaries and Intelligence Summaries are contained in F. S. Regs, Part II. and the Staff Manual respectively. Title pages will be prepared in manuscript.

Hour, Date, Place	Summary of Events and Information	Remarks and References to Appendices
15/1/18 AMBRINES	Lieut E.E. BUNYAN 3rd Lincoln Rgt joined for duty	
16/1/18 do	" E.E. BUNYAN admitted to hospital suffering from gun shot wound in foot (accidental)	
23/1/18 do	Lieut R.H. TURNER, 5th Lincoln Rgt joined for duty. 38 OR joined for duty	
29/1/18 do	Major J.C. LYON assumed command during temporary absence of Lt. Colonel H.B. ROFFEY. D.S.O in command of Brigade. Following officers and 186 OR arrived and taken on strength out of 12 officers and 260 OR posted from 1/4th Lincolnshire Rgt. Lieut H.O. SIMPSON, Lieut. F.R. GIBBON " A.W. WILSON " G. TAYLOR Lieut. E.A. DENNIS " R.G. EEDES " E.G.V. RIGHTON " A.J. ELSTON 2Lieut R.E. CREASEY " C.V. LONGLAND	
31.1.18	The following were mentioned in F.M. Sir D. Haig's despatch dated 15/12/17 Major (T.14 Col) H.B. ROFFEY. 240251 Sgt. FREEMAN F. Capt. G.H. L. HILL (missing). 240074 " HODGSON. O.B. Lieut (a/Capt.) C.N. NEWSUM.	

WAR DIARY
or
INTELLIGENCE SUMMARY.
(Erase heading not required.)

Army Form C. 2118.

Hour, Date, Place	Summary of Events and Information	Remarks and References to Appendices
31/1/15 AMBRINES	Following extracts from London Gazette dated 1/1/15. Awarded D.S.O. Major (T/Lt Colonel). H.B. ROFFEY, Cmdg 2/5/Lincoln Rgt. Awarded D.C.M. 4963 C.S.M. (T/R.S.M.) W. COLDWELL. Lincoln Rgt.	J.C. Lyon, Major Cmdg 2/5th Lincolnshire Regt

Army Form C. 2118.

WAR DIARY
or
INTELLIGENCE SUMMARY.
(Erase heading not required.)

CONFIDENTIAL

WAR DIARY
of the
2/5th Bn. The Lincolnshire Regiment

from 1/2/18 to 28/2/18

Army Form C. 2118.

Instructions regarding War Diaries and Intelligence
Summaries are contained in F.S. Regs., Part II.
and the Staff Manual respectively. Title pages
will be prepared in manuscript.

WAR DIARY
or
INTELLIGENCE SUMMARY.
(Erase heading not required.)

Map References to France Sheet 51c 1/40000. Sheet 51b & 57c 1/10000.

Place	Date	Hour	Summary of Events and Information	Remarks and references to Appendices
AMBRINES I 4 (Sheet	1/2/18 to 9/2/18	-	Major J.C. Lyon in command during absence of Lt. Colonel. H.B. Roffey in temporary command of Brigade. Training was carried out during the period on the lines set out in War Diary for January 1918. Musketry on long and short ranges was carried out and training, firing & Lewis Gun personnel Individual training in the following subjects was given. Bombing, running, scouting and sniping. In addition to consolidate the battalion signalling and first aid. After the reorganisation in a 3 battalion Brigade close order drill was made an outstanding feature in the training together with the practice of field operations for small bodies such as the form & conclusion of the 7 squads training in the new composition of the battalion was well equipped with men in good condition and a fair proportion of Lewis Gunners, bombers, rifle grenadiers &c fit for the support by	fine
GOUY-en-ARTOIS	9/2/18		Bn. marches to GOUY en ARTOIS and went into billets for the night.	fine
BLAIREVILLE	10/2/18		Bn marches to BLAIREVILLE Area and was accommodated in No 4 Camp.	fine
MORY (R.22.SH.57c)	11/2/18		Bn. marches to MORY and was accommodated in MORY South Camp.	fine
BULLECOURT (U.27b.Sh.51b S.W.)	12/2/18		The Bn. relieves the 20th Bn. Middlesex Regt. in the Left Sub Sector of the Centre Brigade front line in the Bullecourt sector and relieves 4 Coys of the 13th Yorkshire Regiment in support in the same sector. The intention is to hold the line firmly but in considerable depth. This Bn. was	fine

Army Form C. 2118.

WAR DIARY
or
INTELLIGENCE SUMMARY.

(Erase heading not required.)

Col. France Sheets 57 S.W. & 57 N.W. Issue

Place	Date	Hour	Summary of Events and Information	Remarks and references to Appendices

BULLECOURT (U.27.b)	12.2.18	—	as strong as the 7 companies relieved.
			The Battalion was disposed as follows:-
			Right Front Company 'A' Coy. Capt G.R. SHERWELL
			   Front Line
			     No 1 Post Lewis Gun. U.22.c.84.45
			     No 2 " " U.22.c.60.40 ⎱ average strength
			     No 3 " " U.22.c.35.45 ⎰ 1 NCO. 12 men
			     No 4 " Lewis Gun U.21.c.1.6
			   Support
			     1 Platoon with Lewis gun at U.25.a antrie. (Beatrix stack post)
			   Reserve
			     1 do with Lewis gun at U.27.b.9.2.
			   Coy H.P. U.27.b.9.2.
			Left Front Company C Coy. Capt A.R. SKIPP
			   Front Line
			     No 5 Post Lewis Gun. U.21.d.8.4.
			     No 6 Post do U.21.d.60.45 ⎱ average strength
			     No 7 " " U.21.d.30.45 ⎰ 1 NCO 12 men
			     No 8 " Lewis gun U.21.d.30.55
			   Surplus men from platoons holding these post are accomodated in (a) CELLAR POST U.21.A.95.15 and (b) in dugout U.21.c.90.75 forming support line cellar post in U.27.b.1.8.
			hd as a strong post
			   Support
			     1 Platoon with Lewis Gun in JOY RIDE SUPPORT U.21.c.70.03 (Cosmetic attack)
			   Reserve
			     1 Platoon with Lewis Gun U.27.b.3.4.
			   Coy H.P. U.27.b.3.4.
				See Appendix I
				See Appendix II

Army Form C. 2118.

WAR DIARY
or
INTELLIGENCE SUMMARY.
(Erase heading not required.)

Ref French Sheets 51b S.W. 1/10000
57c N.W.

Place	Date	Hour	Summary of Events and Information	Remarks and references to Appendices
BULLECOURT (V 27 b)	10/2/18	—	Dispositions (Cont'd)	
			Support Company B. Coy. 2/Lieut. E.A. DENNIS.	
			3 platoons with 2 Lewis guns in TIGER Trench between V.26.c.7.3 and V.26.d.90.85.	
			1 Platoon in STATION Redoubt. V.27.c.15.65.	
			Coy.H.Q. TIGER Trench. V.26.b.7.3.	
			Reserve Company D Coy. Capt. B.H. Challenor.	
			3 platoons in Railway reserve about V.26.c.7.1. 3 Lewis guns holding Nos 11 and 12 Posts at C.2.b.8.4. and C.2.b.5.3. respectively. These posts are permanently garrisoned, being in the front strike line. They are relieved on arrival of Bde reserve troops.	
			1 platoon in Tower Reserve V.27.d.4.4	
			Battalion H.Q. Railway Reserve V.27.d.4.4.	
			Anti aircraft Lewis guns in Tower Reserve V.27.a. and b. 1'r clearing unit.	
			Low flying enemy planes.	
			Unit on left of Bn front. 2/5th Sherwood Foresters join at V.21.d.3.7.	
			" right " " " 2/4th Leicester Regt join at V.22.d.0.6.	
			"Close" touch was maintained with both these units	Yes
			The relief passed off without event.	
— do —	13/2/18	—	Day uneventful. Enemy shelled our line intermittently.	
— do —		8.0 p.m.	Enemy artillery became active and shelled our lines heavily. No casualties. During the night work was carried out in improvement of trenches.	
			Our friendly artillery are friendly speaking in a sad state with much mud of very little use. Front line trenches in better state. Posts very bad.	Yes

Army Form C. 2118.

WAR DIARY
or
INTELLIGENCE SUMMARY.
(Erase heading not required.)

Ref. France Sheets 57d SW / 57c NW } 1/20000

Place	Date	Hour	Summary of Events and Information	Remarks and references to Appendices
BULLECOURT. (V 27 b)	14/2/18		Day uneventful. The enemy's activity was maintained by artillery on both sides. The enemy shelled our trenches with 77mm and 10.5 cm shells. We suffered no casualties. During the night from 9.0 pm onward the enemy's artillery was very active and shelled continuously - at times very heavily - on our support line and about Bn H.Q. No casualties were to arms. Our artillery replied vigorously. Work was continued on improvement of trenches. Wire was erected about V.21c 55.03 in front of Cry R.106 Support for 50ft. This left us to be continued across the front of the front line was accordingly strengthened in night any front trench frontage. This wire is 4ft. Patrolling was carried out in V.21.6 but no enemy were encountered. The enemy's activity seems limited to artillery and his infantry by no means quiet. This pass is no nearer than 500ft from our front line.	[illegible]
—do—	15/2/18		Morning up to about 2.30. It might. Shelling by enemy lighter. Patrols were sent out into V.22.e but no enemy were encountered and has nothing to report. Work on trenches and wiring of Coy Rear Support continued.	[illegible]
	16/2/18 11.45 p.m.		Day and night have been very quiet. Very little artillery activity. Work on trenches and posts was continued. Patrols were sent out during the night.	[illegible]
	17/2/18		But no contact was established with the enemy. Lots sides was freely Situation unchanged. Activity limited to artillery which both sides were freely exchanging and resulted. Work on trenches was continued. Cleaning deepening and revetted.	[illegible]
	18/2/18		B.R. Company relief was carried out. D Company relieving 'A' Coy in the night	

WAR DIARY
or
INTELLIGENCE SUMMARY.
(Erase heading not required.)

Army Form C. 2118.

Ref France Sheet 57c SW 1/40,000
57c N.W 1/40,000

Place	Date	Hour	Summary of Events and Information	Remarks and references to Appendices
BULLECOURT (U 27 b.)	18/2/18	(contd)	Front line. A Coy moving into reserve. B Coy relieves C Coy on the Bn. Front line except that B Coy moving into support. Dispositions were maintained as before the right front company now holds two posts thereabouts held by the Battalion on our right. These are now known as Post 1A U.22.c.90.35 & Lewis gun post. " 1B. U.22.d.1.6.	Yes
– do –	19/2/18		The 9/L Leicester Regiment on our right was relieved by the 4th Lincolnshire Regt. Work on trenches was continued. Situation remained unchanged. On patrols have not succeeded in making a contact with the enemy anywhere within 400 x our front line. Situation unchanged. Work proceeded as usual. There has been severe frost falling in.	Yes
– do –	20/2/18		Enemy was fair about today which must late ordinary H.E. Shells. Five men were affected and sent down. Those shells as different to H.E. marks the enemy to date. The enemy obtained a direct hit on our Lewis gun post 6 (No.10) wounding a Lee boy Kelley two men and wounding three. Lieut Colonel H.B. Coffey D.T.O. handed over command to Major T.C. Lyon on proceeding to command the Brigade during the absence of Lt. Brigadier.	Yes
– do –	21/2/18		Situation unchanged. Working parts and patrols as usual. Enemy artillery fairly active during an support than our; reports of Headquarters. No casualties. Lt. Alston rattley Lt. platoon Coy. was down sent to front line Companies B Coy took over one post No 6 from D Coy otherwise. Dispositions unchanged.	Yes

Army Form C. 2118.

WAR DIARY
or
INTELLIGENCE SUMMARY.
(Erase heading not required.)

Ref. to France _____
Rec'd _____

Place	Date	Hour	Summary of Events and Information	Remarks and references to Appendices
BULLECOURT (U.27.b)	22/2/18 to 24/2/18	—	Situation unchanged. No enemy patrols were encountered. Active enemy patrols to his artillery which shelled our intermittently during the period.	
	24/2/18		Bn. was relieved by 2/4 Bn. Leicestershire Regt. and moved to PASSAGE CAMP, MORY into Brigade Reserve.	
MORY	25/2/18		In Brigade Reserve. Training & Specialist & Lewis Gun and Bombers & Coy. Refresher Drill. Large working parties were found to & trenches to & Trenches Line at E.COURT.	
	26/2/18		Two companies (A & C) were moved to & trenches at C.9.a. "A" Coy to railway embankment at U.26.c.7.1 and trench at C.26.c.7.7, "C" situated near C.9.a.	
			Bn H.Q. and 2 Companies remained at MORY.	
MORY	27/2/18 to 28/2/18		2 companies training at MORY. 2 coys working on trench system in front of and in rear line (from E.COURT). Bn H.Q. B and D Coys moved up relieving the Reserve Coys of 2/4 Lincolnshire Regt in trenches in C.9.a. and 2/4 Leicesters at U.26.c.7.1. Bn. H.Q. established at U.26.c.7.1. The following officers have joined during the month. Lieut. G.R. SPERWELL } from 4 [Inns of Court] O.T.C Lieut. A.H. CHALLENOR } Lieut. P.E. COTTIS } from H.L. march Regt. 2/Lt. H.S. PAYNE " F.J. LEVI " 2/Lt. G.V. BUTLER from A.S.C.	

J. Alexander Capt.
Comdg 2/5 Lincoln Regt.
28/2/18

1/5 Lincolnshire Regt.　　　　Copy No. 12
Operation Order No. 56　　　　8/2/18.

1. The Battn. will move tomorrow by march route to GOUY EN ARTOIS via GIVENCHY - AVESNES LES COMTE - BARLY - FOSSEUX. Starting point X roads I 3 d 1 2. Dress F.S.M.O.

2. First Line Transport will march with the Battn. Lewis Gun limbers followed by Lewis Gun teams march behind their Coys.

3. March discipline will be strictly maintained. Coy Comdrs may see Bde instructions thereon at the Orderly Room.

4. There will be a halt of 10 minutes, 10 minutes before each clock hour.

5. Lewis Gun Limbers will report to their Coys this afternoon to be loaded. Surplus Coy stores will be packed carefully & securely and labelled & handed in to the Q.M. Stores by 8am tomorrow to go on Mechanical Transport.

6. Officers valises will be taken to the Q.M. Stores by 8 am. Blankets, rolled in bundles of 10 & labelled will be taken to the stores at the same time.

7. The following advance party will report at Bde H.Q. at 8am tomorrow

(2)

Lieut H.J. GALE
and one NCO per company.
They will proceed by motor lories from
there & report the Town Major at
GOUY EN ARTOIS and take over
billets.

8. Order of march will be HQ, A.B.C.D. Coys.
HQ will pass starting point at
10 am.

Capt &/Lt
2/5 Lincoln Regt

8.2.18.

Coy
Nos relative
2-6 Coys
7 TO
8 QM
9 MO
10 CO
11-12 War Diary

2/1 Lincolnshire Regt.
Operation Order No. 57   9.2.18

1. The Battn. will move tomorrow by march route to Hendecourt via Le Bac du Sud cross roads Q 27 d 9.9. 5.0 - Basseux - Bellacourt - Boisleux-court. Starting point cross roads Q 19 a 4.4.
   Dress: F.S.M.O.

2. First line Transport will march with the Battn. Lewis Gun Limber followed by their teams will march behind Coys. Pack Ponies as for today.

3. Orders as to march discipline as for today.

4. There will be a halt of 10 minutes before each clock hour.

5. Lewis Gun Limber will be loaded this evening ready to move off with Coys. tomorrow. Surplus stores will be delivered to the Q.M. Stores as for today.

6. Officers valises will be taken to the Q.M. Stores at 6.30 a.m. Blankets rolled tightly in bundles of 10, securely labelled will be taken to the Rail way by 8 a.m.

7. The following advance party will parade at Regade H.Q. (The Chateau in this village) at 8 a.m. where a lorry will convey them to Hendecourt where they will take over camps ready for

this unit:-
      2Lt H.J.GALE
      1 NCO per coy.
Baggage. 4 Lembers will be at Bde
HQ at the Chateau in this village at
9 am tomorrow. The Quartermaster
will send a guide to bring the lorries
to the QM Stores.
8. Order of march will be HQ. A B C
D Coy. HQ will pass the starting
point at 10.5 am.

2/5 Lincolnshire Regt.
Operation Order No. 68.   10/2/18.
Map Sheets 57°C & 57°NW.

1. The Battn. will move tomorrow by march route to a camp at MORY. Map reference of camp B.22.o.5.4.(57°C) via Hendecourt - Boiry-St-Martin. Starting Point - road junction X.17.b.4.6.(57°C) over H.Q. Steel helmets will be worn.

2. First line transport will march with the Battn. as far as Hamelincourt.

3. Lewis Gun limbers will march as for today with team behind each Kitchen will also follow their Coys. Pack ponies will not proceed beyond the road junction at S.29.a.9.2. but will wait for Transport Officer instructions. Water Cart & Medical Cart will proceed to move.

4. There will be a halt of 10 minutes before each clock hour.

5. Lewis Gun limbers will be loaded this evening ready to move off with Coys tomorrow. Surplus stores will be delivered as for today to the QMr.

6. Officers valises & blankets rolled tightly in bundles of 10 will be delivered to the Quartermaster Stores by 8.0 a.m.

7. An advance party of 2 N.C.Os. and

one NCO per Coy will proceed to the camp at MORY to take over, leaving here at 9.30 am. No lorry is available and the QM will obtain 5 bicycles from the Signallers for this party. 'X' Baton of the 18th Welsh Bttn. is at present at MORY.

8. Baggage. Only 2 lorries are available tomorrow. The QM will send guides to Bde SH2 in Quarry R 34 d for these lorries at 5 am tomorrow. Pack up officers valises & those necessary to the Battn will be taken on the first trip to MORY leaving behind those things which will only be required at the Transport lines in HAMELINCOURT.

9. Order of march will be HQ A B C D Coys. Intervals of 200x will be maintained between Coys. HQ will pass starting point at 10.15 am.

10/2/18.

Capt & Adjt
2/5 Lincoln Regt.

2/5 Lincolnshire Regt.
Operation Order No. 54   12/2/18

1. The Battn will relieve the 20th Middlesex Regt in the front line of the sub-sector of the Bullecourt Centre Brigade tonight & also the support & reserve of the left sub-sector now held by the 13th Yorkshire Regt.

2. A Coy 2/5 Lincolns will take the right front line coy & right support, relieving B coy & C coy of the 20th Middlesex. C coy will take the left front line & left support coy, relieving A and C coy of the 20th Middlesex. B Coy will relieve one coy of the 13th Yorks Regt. becoming support company. D coy will relieve 2 coys of the 13th Yorks becoming reserve coy.

3. Guides, one to white [?] proceed to coy comdrs will be at the cross road B.17.d.23 at 5 p.m. tonight.

4. The following transport will accompany the Battn. Cyclists, Lewis Gun limbers [?] detached the Lewis gun pickaxe cart & coy Lmg limber, pack animals, gas [?] cart, H.Q. water tins with rations. Remainder cart will remain behind at H.Q.

5. Guides will be able to inform Coys to what front they are to take their numbers.

6. The Baton will pass at 4.25 p.m. to the troops & will march out in Platoons or corresponding bodies at 100ᵡ intervals. Order of march A.B.C.D.HQ. All details for posts must be arranged beforehand & named in the order in which they will be required as they move up into the line.

7. B.Coy will have 1 NCO 3 men & a Lewis Gun with panniers spare parts bag etc. to A.coy. D.Coy will make a similar loan to C. coy.

8. Rations for consumption on the 13ᵗʰ will be carried on the men. B & D Coys will carry one Blanket per man. All other Blankets, Officers valises, spare Lewis Gun boxes & all other Coy stores not required will be dumped at the Guard Tent as soon as possible & not later than 2.15 p.m.

9. All trench stores & maps will be taken over.

   ✗ Administrative instructions for the line will be issued later.

10. Coys will forward by 5 p.m. 13ᵗʰ inst. a complete list with map references showing their dispositions giving accurate positions of post Lewis Guns & H.Q.

11. The code Word 'PALERME' will be
used to Battn HQ on comp[letion] of
actn[?]

12.3.15   [?]
                           O/C [?] Regt

b/y
No 1 [?]
  [?] [?]
  7   TO
  8   QM
  9   MO
  10 RSM
  11 & 12 War Diary

Operation Orders No 6. 19/7/15

The following inter Coy relief will take place tomorrow night 18th inst. D Coy will relieve A Coy in the right front Line.
B Coy will relieve C Coy in their front Line.

2. All details of relief will be arranged between Coy Comdrs concerned.

3. All Trench & Area Stores will be handed over.

4. O/C A Coy will arrange to leave 2 Lewis Gun Teams with Guns in the Line for the use of D Coy. The present Gun Team of B Coy attached to A Coy will rejoin it's own Coy after relief tomorrow, when they will be placed with the reserve platoon. O.C. C Coy will leave in the line for B Coy. The present Team of D Coy attached to C Coy will rejoin it's own Coy in the Lines after relief, where it will be placed with the reserve platoon. Coy Comdrs of B & D Coys should visit their respective fronts today & make arrangements for runners &c to be sent up to learn runner routes, Trenches &c.

Completion of relief will be reported

to H.Q by the code word wire.

17/7/18   Capt A.M.
                                           2/5 Leinster Regt

1 Retained
2&5 Coys
6   H.Q
7   R.S.M
8   T.O
9   M.O
10 Q.M
11&12 War Diary

Operation Order 26/7/18

Ref to France Sheets 57c NW & 51b SW

1. The Bn will be relieved in the left Sub Sector of the Bullecourt Sector tomorrow night 27/7/18 by the 4th Lancashire Regiment.

2. The following guides will be provided:- 1 all Coy, 1 for Coy HQ & 1 per platoon Bn HQ 1 guide.

3. Guides will report at Bn HQ at 5.0 pm tomorrow 27/7/18, Rendezvous with 4th Lancashire guides at U.27.d.9.2. (road junction)

4. All trench & other Stores as taken over from previous units will be handed over.

(a) All petrol Tins.
(b) All Boilers Dixies & Fixers.
(c) Ammunition previous S.A.A. & Tracer will not be handed over.
(d) The Regimental Hot Tea Containers will not be handed over, but Ordnance pattern containers will be handed over.

5. The following transport will be available at points shewn. 8.30 pm. A Coy, 1 Limber for Lewis Gun Etc at C.1.d.9.1. 8.30 pm.

B, C & D Coys 1 Limber each
at A.27.d.10.4.
H.Q. Sufficient transport for H.Qrs
& R.A.P. at A.27.d.0.4.
A Lewis Gun section will march
with each Limber.

6. Coys in relief will ~~march~~ proceed
to MORY ABBAYE Camp independently
by & by platoon at intervals of 100 yards
distance. Hot Soup etc will be
available.

7. A Coy & O/C H.Q. Coy will each send
one Lewis gun to report to Ammunition
Dump at B.26.a. for Anti-Aircraft
work relieving guns of 4th Leicesters
there. H.Q. Swill supply 3 Men, O/C
A Coy, 1 N.C.O. & 4 Men for this duty.
Meet at A Coys H.Q.s at 9.0 am
& proceed with guns to dumps direct.
4 Magazines per gun will be taken.

8. Completion of relief will be reported
by code words O.K. M.S.

23/2/18

Capt & Adjt
5/Lincoln Regt

15th Bn 2nd Infe Bde 27/2/18
Warning Order

1. The Battn. less two companies will move to the ECOUST area tomorrow. Start time about 4.0 pm.

2. Lewis Gun Limbers will be packed in camp at 2.0 pm.

3. 45 men will be required from each of B & D Coys for working parties tomorrow night. Details will be communicated.
Arrangements will be made for packs of the men to be taken to Ecoust. They themselves will proceed from YTRES to Ecoust on ___

4. Transport required
   Lewis Gun Limbers
   2 Limbers for H.Q.
   Officers' Cart (for RAP & Mess)
   2 Limbers for Blankets

5. QM will make necessary arrangements for looks & rations & details to be discussed to Mess. Stores tomorrow. Rations will be carried up in both & if additional transport is required

T.O. [illegible]

27/2/18   2/5 Lincoln Rgt

59th Division.
177th Infantry Brigade.

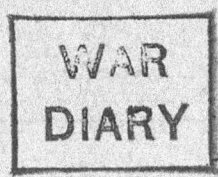

2/5th BATTALION

THE LINCOLNSHIRE REGIMENT

MARCH 1918

Attached - Report on Operations 21st - 25th March

Army Form C. 2118.

WAR DIARY
or
INTELLIGENCE SUMMARY.

(Erase heading not required.)

Original 1/59

172

Place	Date	Hour	Summary of Events and Information	Remarks and references to Appendices

CONFIDENTIAL

War Diary of the 2/5th Bn
The LINCOLNSHIRE Regt

from 1/3/15 to 31/3/15

1/4/15

H.M. Duffy Lieut Colonel
Comdg 2/5th Bn Lincolnshire Regt

Army Form C. 2118.

WAR DIARY
or
INTELLIGENCE SUMMARY.
(Erase heading not required.)

Map Ref FRANCE Sheets 51b SW } 1/10000
57 c N.W.

Instructions regarding War Diaries and Intelligence Summaries are contained in F. S. Regs., Part II. and the Staff Manual respectively. Title pages will be prepared in manuscript.

Place	Date	Hour	Summary of Events and Information	Remarks and references to Appendices
ECOUST ST. MEIN C2 (57c NW)	1/3/18		Battalion was in Brigade Reserve. H.Q. and 2 companies in Railway Embankment U.26 C.7.1 2 companies in Sunken Road and trench between ECOUST and NOREUIL about C.3.c.7.0. Working parties furnished by day and night.	
BULLECOURT (V27 S16.SW)	2/3/18		Bn relieved the 4th LINCOLNSHIRE Regt in the right sub sector of the Brigade Sector and was disposed as follows:- Right Front Line Coy.(A) Held front line by series of Posts at V.29.a.4.9. V.23.d.5.1. V.23.d.15.30. V.23.d.80.35 with Support posts in rear. One platoon for counter attack at V.29.c.8.2 (TANK AVENUE) Coy HQ V.27 c.9.5.95. Left Front Line Coy (C) Held front line by series of posts at V.22.R.70.40, V.2?2.d.4.7. V.22.d.30.65 with a right post at V.22.d.2.6. Support posts distributed along FOX RIDE SUPPORT V.22.d.5.3. One platoon for counter attack at Coy HQ at V.23.c.55.95. (LONDON RESERVE) Support Coy (D) One platoon in FOX TROT SUPPORT at V.27.6.7.7. Two platoons in GORDON RESERVE at V.25.a.3.2 Bn HQ and One Reserve Coy (B) in RAILWAY RESERVE at V.25.c.9.2. 2 RAILWAY RESERVE at V.25.c.7.3. Unit on right 2/6 SOUTH STAFFORDS Rgt. " Left 2/4th LEICESTER Rgt. The general policy of defence was to hold the main line of resistance viz. FOX TROT – FOX TROT SUPPORT. Anything nearer from line post only made in case of small raids by enemy not in the Big attack. General attack of enemy was successful and if the right from on our attempt at Patronella was repeatedly made by the Germans, the front line only a few yards apart. Such attacks were always repulsed & did not enable the German patrols to do anything for	

Army Form C. 2118.

WAR DIARY
or
INTELLIGENCE SUMMARY.

1/4 Bn. Rif. FRANCE Sheet 57d SW } 1/20,000
57d NW } 1/20,000

(Erase heading not required.)

Instructions regarding War Diaries and Intelligence Summaries are contained in F. S. Regs., Part II. and the Staff Manual respectively. Title pages will be prepared in manuscript.

Place	Date	Hour	Summary of Events and Information	Remarks and references to Appendices
BULLECOURT (U.27 S1 b5 w)	2/3/18	—	Enemy busy offering our own Eparith etc in exchange of the numbers of German units opposite. A few days activity on the part of our snipers reduced the numbers of German units considerably.	few
— do —	3/3/18	—	Situation quiet. Enemy activity equals to our artillery. Shells down intermittently. Owing to a suspected enemy offensive our patrols have very active especially before dawn. German prisoners all declare that an attack will be made shortly against this sector. There are some indications on the German line of the...	few
— do —	5/3/18	5·0 pm	A raid on the enemy trenches at U.23.c.2.5 was made by a party of the 4th LINCOLNSHIRE Regt. was carried out. The enemy front line trench was found empty so through the German two lines. It is stated that this area is occupied only at Daniel German posts and views to curve up a case to suspected. Two men only of our ranks. Major H.WARD Lincoln & Major B. [...] rejoined. A coy moving into [...] in forward.	few
— do —	6/3/18	—	Inter company relief. B Coy relieved A Coy. D Coy relieved C Coy. Into support. C Coy into reserve. D [...] unchanged. The weather has chiefly been wet and the trenches are considerably improved. Work has chiefly been ordinary [...] They have never re-opened JOY RIDE SAP and [...] for days on the communication trenches. Trenches have been cleared of mud and good water to is now good.	few
— do —	7/3/18 to 12/3/18	—	Situation unchanged. Work on trenches and putting the new forward and S JOY RIDE support in U.22.c has been made. None are no counting indications of an enemy offensive. It has out out a few days the enemy will have plans and countering are too days ago state that the attack will take place at 13 not [...]	few
— do —	13/3/18	—	2 pairs of the German Artillery a heavy artillery emg counter preparation	few

Army Form C. 2118.

WAR DIARY
or
INTELLIGENCE SUMMARY
(Erase heading not required.)

Maj. Reg. FRANCE.   5/6 Inn.
                      5/6 N. Staffs

Place	Date	Hour	Summary of Events and Information	Remarks and references to Appendices
BULLECOURT (U.27, S.9, S.16, S.M)	13/3/18		Was carried out during the night 12/13. The enemy's trenches heavily shelled & swept by M.G. fire throughout the night. No attempt on attack. Enemy approached wire assembling for an attack. No attempt to force them from the enemy's front line silently and was seen to be carried out. The enemy's trenches enveloped and as usual. We had one man wounded. The enemy gave one German post exhibited a more marked business as usual.	✓
	14/3/18		Weather favourable. Was carried out on the night 13/3/13 but came to grief to some extent. Day was very quiet. A few enemy shells fell on our line. The Bn. was relieved by the 2/4 LEICESTER Regt. and moved back into Brigade Reserve. HQ and 2 Coys. at U.26.c.7.1. 2 Coys. at C.2.c.7.0. 2 Brigade Reserve Carrying parties were found day and night to work on new defences, cable trenches & dugouts. Men were taken to Coys. etc. Enemy intermittently on different fronts. Enemy shelled on ECOUST.	✓ ✓
ECOUST ST MEIN C.2 (57c.N.W.)	15/3/18 to 18/3/18			✓
	19/3/18 to 20/3/18		Relieved by 1/6 N. STAFFS Regt and moved to MORY on DUNMAIL Camp accommodated at MORY SOUTH CAMP. Owing to suspected enemy attack important the Battalion stands to each morning one hour before day break.	✓
	21/3/18 to 26/3/18		See special account of operations during this period attacked.	✓ ✓
SUS ST LEGER	27/3/18		Bn moved by march route to SUS ST LEGER.	✓ ✓
	29/3/18		" " " to HOUDAIN entraining at PREVENT.	

Army Form C. 2118.

WAR DIARY
or
INTELLIGENCE SUMMARY.
(Erase heading not required.)

Place	Date	Hour	Summary of Events and Information	Remarks and references to Appendices
HOUDAIN	30/3/18		Accommodated in billets. Reorganisation of Coys commenced.	
—do—	31/3/18		Draft of 1 officer (2Lieut. L.W.H. HAWKINS) and 31 O.R. arrived. The following officers have been struck off the strength during the month.	
			Lieut. E.G. BUTLER. Sick to England	
			2Lieut. A.R. LUNN do do	
			" J. COX do do	
			Lieut. M.T. CHAMBERS England War worn 21.3.18	
			" H.S. PAYNE do 31.3.17	
			Lieut (A/Capt) B.H. CHALLONER Missing in action 21/3/18 2Lieut F. SHARPE Missing in action 21.3.18	
			Capt. E.J.R. HETT do 21/3/18 " W.T. ALLEN do 21.3.18	
			2Lieut (a/Capt) A. BEGG. (Norfolk Rgt) do 21/3/18 a/Major (A/Capt.) H. WARD. Killed do 21.3.18	
			2Lieut. N.J. GALE do 21/3/17 Lieut. G.V. BUTLER. A.S.C. 23.3.18	
			2Lieut. L.G. MOSS do 21/3/18 Lieut. R.H. TURNER Wounded 21.3.18	
			" F.J. LEVI. do 21/3/18 2Lieut R.G. GEDIS do 21.3.18	
			" P.E. COTTIS. do 21/3/18 " F.B. SMITH do 21.3.18	
			" F.R. GIBBONS do 21/3/18 " E.G. TAYLOR do 21.3.18	
			" R.E. CREASEY do 21.3.18	
			Capt. L.M. WEBBER RAMC do 21.3.18	
			2Lieut A.J. ELSTON Missing 21.3.18	
			4963 R.S.M. W. COLDWELL (appendices 21.3.18) and 497 OR.	

K.M. ?
Lieut Colonel
Cmdg 2/5th Lincoln Rgt

An Account of the Part taken by
the 7/5th Bn. the LINCOLNSHIRE Regt in
the German Offensive commencing
on 21st March 1918.

Ref. Special Map attached.

21.3.18 On the 21st March 1918 the Bn. was part
MORY of the Brigade in Reserve to the 59th Division
4.0 am and was in camp at MORY.
Intermittent gunfire throughout the
night increasing in violence. There about
4.0 am there was no doubt that
something was happening on the front
line. Bn. was ordered to "Stand To"
and shortly afterwards orders to that
effect were received from 177 Bde.

7.0 am At 7.0 am the Bn. was ordered to
advance at once to the Assembly
position in B.24.a. The move was
completed and the Bn. formed up in

7.36 am artillery formation by 7.36 am.

8.50 am Patrols were sent out at 8.50 am
under 2/Lieuts. E.A. DENNIS and F. SHARPE
along ECOUST SPUR and Track to
VRAUCOURT COPSE respectively. These
patrols reported heavy shelling of
ECOUST and on firing and Support
lines of 3rd System. Also a runner
of 178 Bde informed them that an
enemy infantry attack had developed

21.3.18. by 9.0 am in the front System.
12.0 noon. At 12.400N the Bn was ordered to advance and occupy the Support trench of the First Battle System in C.9. The 4 Leicester Regt was to be on our left. The Bn advanced along Track 3 under thro' the wire of the 2nd Battle System, & there extended into artillery formation A Coy on right leading roughly along the NOREUIL SWITCH, B C & D Coys extending to the left, Bn H.Q. being 200x in rear.

On Bn H.Q. passing the wire of the front line 3rd System it was noticed that the Coys were apparently easing too much to the right and orders were about to be sent to rectify this. During the whole of this advance the Bn was under heavy artillery and M.g. fire. Several officers were wounded including Lieuts. R. GEEDES F.B. SMITH and G TAYLOR. and R.S.M. W. COLDWELL.

When Bn H.Q. arrived above C.14.b.O.t. the cause of the Coys drawing to the right was apparent. Large masses of enemy were seen streaming over the ridge to the S.E. of LONGATTE

21.3.18 and they were already in possession of their objective. Seeing this it appears that the company commanders decided that the best thing to do was to man the NOREUIL SWITCH and thus outflank the enemy. The CO decided to also man the NOREUIL SWITCH, with Bn HQ & 2 platoons of D Coy which were a little behind the front line, in C.14.b.

12.20 pm An officer patrol under 2nd Lieut R.E. CREASEY was sent along the NOREUIL SWITCH to get in touch with the remainder of the Bn. He had not gone far when he met parties of the enemy in between BHQ and the Coys in front. He and most of the patrol were wounded. At this time it was observed that large bodies of enemy troops were advancing from NOREUIL up the HIRONDELLE VALLEY and on the Spur beyond. Seeing this the CO. decided to man the firing line of the 3rd System in C.14.C. Owing to the shape of the ground it was impossible to see what was happening to the rest of the Bn. A patrol was sent out under Sergt. WHATMOUGH along the NOREUIL SWITCH to try to find the position of the Coys in front & to establish the enemy's dispositions. This patrol could not proceed as they

21.3.18

nil large enemy forces; and neither could they see anything of the companies in front.

12.15 pm On arriving at the firing line of the 3rd System it was found that the 4th LINCOLN Regt were holding it to our left but there was a considerable gap which was closed with the few troops available. Major G.H. Deane of the 4th Lincolns came over & reported the situation and dispositions of his unit. No information was received as to the position of the 2/4 Leicester Regt.

The enemy in the meantime appeared to be moving in large numbers across our front from right to left and getting into the valley in C.14 a and b. These were engaged by our 2 remaining Lewis Guns and with rifle fire. They reached the wire in front of us but were beaten off.

Major H. WARD was sent off to the left to get to know the location of the 4 Leicester Regt. He was unfortunately killed in so doing.

3.0 pm At this time Sergt. GARNHAM, who was commanding the extreme right platoon about the junction of the NOREUIL SWITCH with the firing line 3rd System, reported the presence of the enemy

21/3/18 in considerable numbers in VRAUCOURT COPSE. He states that his Lewis gun and rifle fire did considerable execution. A message was sent to Bde H.Q. to inform artillery.

3.15 pm. It was now decided to move Bn HQ from the firing line to the support line. It moved along the firing line of the 3rd System until the ECOUST-BEUNATRE road at which point the O.C. 4 LEICESTERS was met who gave the situation on the left flank. Bn H.Q. moved down the road towards support line 3rd System and met O.C. 4 LINCOLNS about B.24.b.8.6. and it was agreed to form a joint Bn H.Q. at C.19.a.3.5

5.0 pm. A patrol was now sent out under Sergt. WHATMOUGH to creep along the HIRONDELLE VALLEY. Patrol reports that it could not proceed beyond C.20.a.7.7. owing to heavy m.g. and rifle fire from VRAUCOURT COPSE.

Capt. L.M. WEBBER R.A.M.C.(T). M.O. i/c Bn. had established his aid post in the front line at the beginning of the battle. This was necessary as there was no chance of casualties reaching him until dark if the aid post had been further back, &

21.3.18

many of the wounded officers and men were in need of more attention than could be given by stretcher bearers. He carried out his duties in a most gallant manner until he himself was severely wounded.

5.20pm. At this time it appeared that our right flank was in danger of being turned and troops were asked for to fill up the gap between our right and the left of the 6th Division on our right. A Pioneer Bn, 6/7 Roy. Scots. Fus. was sent up for this purpose.

8.0pm. Orders were received that the Bde would be relieved in the Front Line by the 14 Argyle and Sutherland Highlanders & HLI, & that 177th Bde would occupy the Support line of the 3rd System. 4 Lincolns on right, 5 Lincolns Centre and 4 Leicesters on left.

22.3.18 Relief was completed at 5.0 am. Bn was holding support line from B24b.9.8. to B24b.3.6. Bn HQ at B x8 & 3x 24d.9.8.

The Bn now consisted of Lieut. Colonel. H.B. ROFFEY D.S.O, Capt & Asst J.C. URQUHART, Lieuts. E.A. DENNIS, W.A. BALL E.G.V. RIGHTON and about 80 NCOs and men.

22.3.18. During the morning and early afternoon the enemy seemed to be pushing towards VRAUCOURT on our right. The situation on our front appeared good and the men were well entrenched.

3.45pm About 3.45pm a message was received from Bde saying that the enemy were in VRAUCOURT and at the same time a report came in that the enemy were in the firing line of the 3rd System (of the 128th Bde). The troops in the firing line 3rd System came back and those in the Support line began to withdraw also. The men of 177 Infy Bde were collected and reestablished themselves in their former positions. The 2/5th Lincolns were collected in road at B.24 b 5.1. and acted as general reserve.

5.30pm About 5.30pm the last of our troops were driven out of VRAUCOURT on our right. The capture of this village by the enemy rendered our position untenable. In consultation with O.C. 4 Lincolns it was decided to withdraw to the firing line of the 4th System. This withdrawal

7.30pm was carried out, and at dusk the Bn was dug in in the 4th System in B.23.a. on a front of about 300x.

22/3/18 4 Lincolns were on the right and 2/4 Leicesters on the left.

8.0 pm About 8.0 pm an officer from the 2/4 Leicesters Regt came in breathless & stated that he had been sent from his regiment to say that the troops of the Division on the left had been driven in and that the enemy had got round the flank of the 2/4 Leicesters and was almost into MORY. He also reported that the 2/4 Leicesters were withdrawing to the ARRAS-BAPAUME Rd. At this time the enemy were shooting into the backs of our men and it was decided to withdraw round the S. Side of MORY. This was done and on arriving at B.27 a. Central the Bn was halted and the CO. proceeded to DYSART CAMP to report to Bde H.Q. 4 LINCOLNS halted at the same place the whereabouts of the 2/4 Leicesters being unknown. Orders were received from Bde to try and re-establish our line on the 4th System and arrangements were made for the 2/4th Leicesters to advance through MORY and 2/5th and 4th Lincolns on right of MORY.

11.30 pm This operation was attempted

22.3.18	but MORY was held too strongly by the enemy and the 2/4 Leicesters were unable
23.3.18	to advance. The 2/4 Leicesters established
1.0 am	themselves in the centre of MORY. O.C. 4/5 Lincolns decided to take up a defensive position on high ground in B.27.b. in a series of posts sited & constructed so as to be able to fire towards MORY and also to the EAST. 4th Lincolns took up a defensive position in Sunken road about B.27 central.
6.20 am	Orders were received to withdraw and occupy Spur in B.20 facing MORY. This withdrawal was carried out under heavy m.g. and artillery fire from direction of MORY, and the Bn dug in on the line B.20.c.3.0. to B.20.c.5.6. with Bn H.Q at B.25.b.8.8. 4 Lincolns were on right and 2/4 Leicesters on left. The day passed fairly quietly. Our position and trenches were improved and supplies of S.A.A. and water were carried forward to the posts.
24.3.18	During the night our trenches were heavily shelled by our own guns and those of the enemy. Repeated messages were sent to Bde asking

24.3.18	Artillery to lengthen range. The 2/4th Leicesters were attacked during the night in rear of MORY and although they made a gallant counter attack the enemy succeeded in capturing their trenches early on the morning of 25.3.18. The line of the 4th and 2/5 Lincolns was still intact but the left was considerably exposed. Trenches were at once constructed to cover our left flank and touch was established with the remnants of British troops holding out in ERVILLERS.
9.0 am to 1.0 pm	During the morning the enemy had been seen debauching from MORY and in the early afternoon large numbers were seen advancing over the ridges on either side of MORY.
3.0 pm	About 3.0 pm a message was received from O.C. 4th Lincolns to the effect that he was withdrawing to form a defensive flank facing BEHAGNIES as the troops on his right had fallen back and the enemy was in possession of BEHAGNIES. This left the Bn with both flanks exposed.
3.30 pm	The CO about 3.30 pm decided that as both flanks were gone & the men were very exhausted that it

24.3.18 would be impossible for the Bn to maintain its position and so ordered a withdrawal to trenches about 600x E of GOMIECOURT.

5.0pm Orders were now received that the Bn would be relieved by the E. LANCS Regt. This was carried out and the Bn withdrew during the night to

25.3.18 BOCQUOY. arriving there at 3.0 am on
3.0am 25.3.18. ?(26")

4.30 " Orders received to move at once to Le QUESNOY FARM where it arrived at 6.30 am The Transport & Q 17 stores were found to be established here.

9.30am Bn marched out for SAILLY au BOIS. On arrival at FONQUEVILLERS, information was received that the enemy were at SAILLY au BOIS and HEBUTERNE and the Bde halted and occupied trenches facing HEBUTERNE and (SAILLY AU BOIS). In the afternoon the situation had apparently cleared and orders were received to march to BIENVILLERS.

The following casualties were incurred during this fighting.
Killed Lt Capt (A/Major) H. WARD   21.3.18
        Lieut. G.V. BUTLER A.S.C   23.3.18.
Wounded. Lieut. R.H. TURNER   21.3.18

Wounded (contd)
    2nd Lieut. R. G. EEDES   21.3.18
          "   R. E. CREASEY   do
          "   F. B. SMITH   do
          "   G. TAYLOR   do
    Capt. L. M. WEBBER R.A.M.C.(T).   do.

Missing
    Capt. E. J. R. HETT.   21.3.18
    Lieut. (a/Capt.) B. H. CHALLENOR.   do
    2/Lieut. (a/Capt.) A. BEGG. (4 Norfolks) do
          "   H. J. GALE   do
          "   F. SHARPE   do
          "   F. R. GIBBONS   do
          "   F. & J. LEVI   do
          "   P. E. COTTIS M.C.   do
          "   L. G. MOSS   do
          "   G. W. ALLEN   do
Wounded   "   A. J. ELSTON   do.
    4963 R.S.M. W. COLDWELL   do.

O.R. Killed, wounded & missing
estimated at 490.   } 21.3.18
                            to
                            25.3.18

                            [signature]
                            Lieut. Colonel
                            Cmdg. 2/5 Lincoln Regt

30/3/18

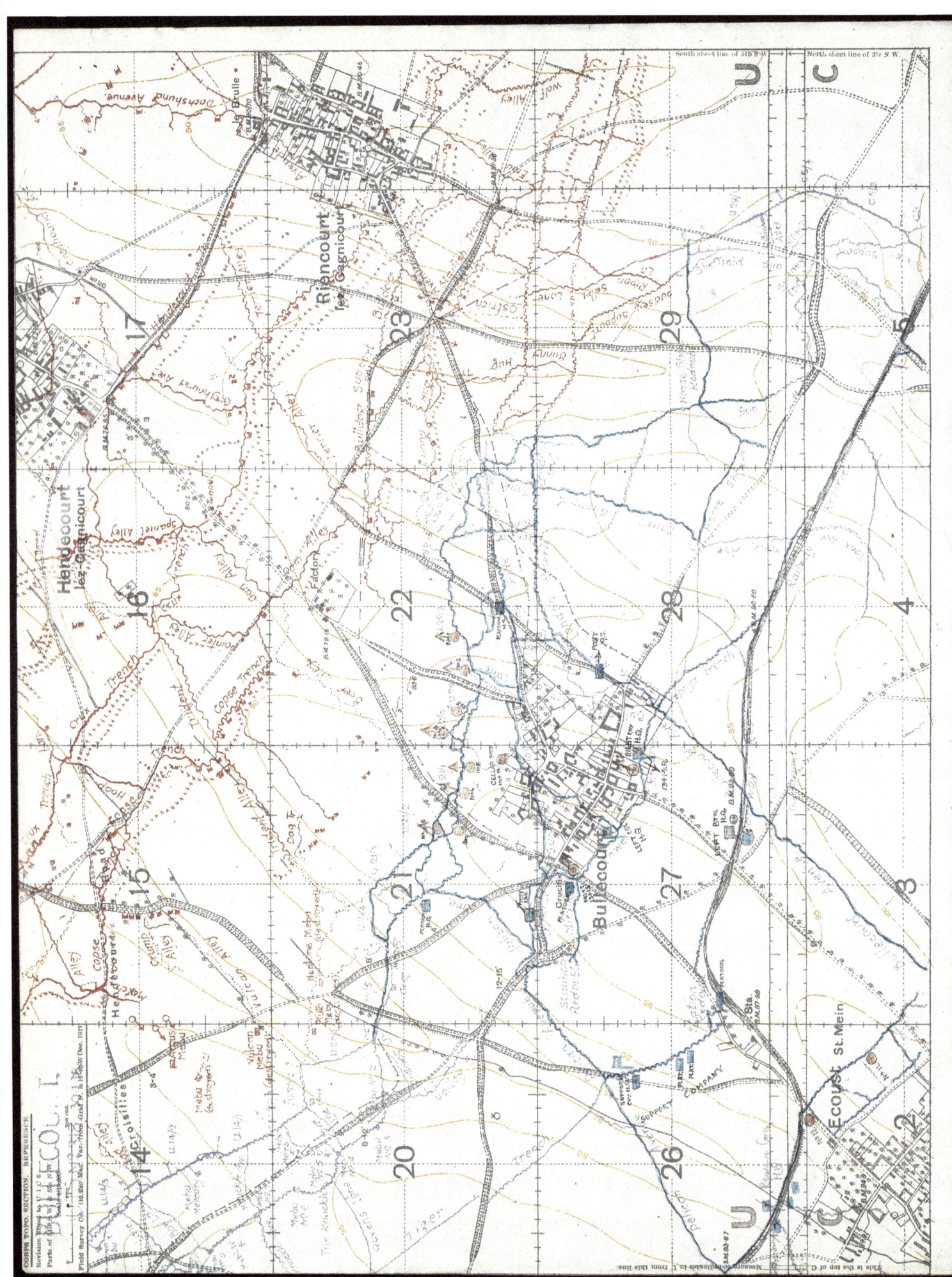

177th Brigade.

59th Division.

2/5th BATTALION

LINCOLNSHIRE REGIMENT

APRIL 1918.

Army Form C. 2118.

WAR DIARY
or
INTELLIGENCE SUMMARY.
(Erase heading not required.)

172/59

Vol 15

CONFIDENTIAL

WAR DIARY

of the

1/5th Bn. the LINCOLNSHIRE REGT.

from

1/4/15 to 30/4/15

1/5/15

J Ansell?
Col. 1/5 Linc Rt

Army Form C. 2118.

WAR DIARY
or
INTELLIGENCE SUMMARY.
(Erase heading not required.) BELGIUM & FRANCE Ref Sheets 27 and 28 F.

Instructions regarding War Diaries and Intelligence Summaries are contained in F. S. Regs., Part II. and the Staff Manual respectively. Title pages will be prepared in manuscript.

Place	Date	Hour	Summary of Events and Information	Remarks and references to Appendices
HOUDAIN	1/4/18		Entrained at HOUDAIN for PROVEN where in detrained and marched to a camp at ST JANSTER BIEZEN near WATOU	
WATOU	1/4/18 to 4/4/18		Reorganisation and refitting. Drafts were constantly received during this period but no officers were included. The fixed strength of the battalion not being or deficiencies of stores and equipment were made up. A fair percentage of Lewis gunners and signallers were included in the drafts.	
ZONNEBEKE	4/4/18		Bn relieved the GLASGOW HIGHLANDERS (9th H.L.Infy) in the Left subsector of the ZONNEBEKE sector and were disposed as follows. (References to FRANCE Sheet 28 NE) Regt front line Coy - "D" Coy. Lieut J.C Myers 4 advanced posts of 1 NCO & 6 men between D.23.c.95.60 and D.23.a.70.20. 3 Support posts of 1 NCO, 1 platoon each at D.23.c.0.6. D.23.c.0.9 and D.23.a.10.25 Coy H.Q. D.23.c.0.9. Left front line Coy. C Coy. Capt A.R.W. SKIPP. 4 advanced posts of 1 NCO + 6 men between D.23.a.70.20 and D.23.a.50.90. Support posts of 2 platoons at D.23.a.27. " 1 " at D.17.c.40.15 Coy H.Q. D.17.c.40.15 Regt Support Coy B Coy. Lieut L.W.M HAWKINS. 2 platoon at MOULIN FARM. D.22.a.S.5. 2 platoons at CORDIALE FACTORY. D.21.d.95.20 Coy H.Q. do D.21.d.95.20 Left Support Coy. 2 platoons + Coy H.Q. at D.22.b.85.90 1 platoon at D.22.c.70.30. 1 platoon at THAMES. D.22.c.40.50. Bn H.Q. CORDIALE FACTORY. D.21.d.95.20.	

Army Form C. 2118.

WAR DIARY
or
INTELLIGENCE SUMMARY.
(Erase heading not required.)

Ref. France, Belgium. Sheet 28 N.E. 1/20000

Instructions regarding War Diaries and Intelligence Summaries are contained in F. S. Regs., Part II. and the Staff Manual respectively. Title pages will be prepared in manuscript.

Place	Date	Hour	Summary of Events and Information	Remarks and references to Appendices
ZONNEBEKE	9/4/15	—	Enemy activity chiefly limited to artillery. Nomansland was at least a thousand yards wide at this point. During the day there was no hostile patrols were encountered. Nomansland was very misty and much cut up by shellfire made patrolling difficult. Standing patrols were sent out each night to E. edge of DAISY and DAIRY WOODS. Many of the men were new to the line and there 5 days duty was most to fit them for the fighting which followed. No casualties suffered.	—
—do—	10/4/15		Relieved in line by 2/4th Leicester Regt. Battalion moved to Rear position. Was disposed as follows:— 1 Company ('B' Coy) at D.21.d.9.5.20 to man Divisional Ridge D.22 C.30 (Sheet 28 N.W). 1 Company in Rifle Pits ... Batt H.Q and 2 Companies at ST JEAN CAMP I.36.central (Sheet 28 NW)	Jm
ST JEAN	10/4/15 to 12/4/15		Remained in reserve at ST JEAN Camp. Training & Battling & bathing and interior economy. Bathing at	Jm
—do—	12/4/15		Bn withdrew after troops of 46th Division had taken up position in the Army Line about C.30 (Sheet 28 N.W) and marched to BRANDHOEK CAMP G.11.c.7.2.(do) to BRANDHOEK to EERE	Jm
BRANDHOEK	13/4/15	4.30 pm	Bn entrained and detrained at GODEWAERSVELDE (Q.17.a. Sheet 27) thence at MONT des CATS	Jm
MONT des CATS	14/4/15	12.0am	Bn marched to LOCRE (N.23.c. Sheet 28) where it was temporarily accommodated in huts at 4.50 am	Jm
LOCRE	—do—	11.0 am	Bn moved out along the LOCRE - DRANOUTRE road to about M.29.c. where it cleared the road and awaited orders. The CO and Coy Comd. went forward to reconnoitre the winter line. S.E. DRANOUTRE	Jm

(A5009) D. D. & L., London, E.C. Wt. W1771/M2 31. 750,000 5/17 Sch. 52 Forms/C2118/4.

Army Form C. 2118.

WAR DIARY
or
INTELLIGENCE SUMMARY.
(Erase heading not required.)

Ref. to FRANCE Sheet 28 S.W. 1/20000

Instructions regarding War Diaries and Intelligence Summaries are contained in F. S. Regs., Part II. and the Staff Manual respectively. Title pages will be prepared in manuscript.

Place	Date	Hour	Summary of Events and Information	Remarks and references to Appendices
LOCRE (M.29.c)	14/4/18		Orders were received to relieve the 88th Inf. Bde in the line in REVELSBURG RIDGE in S.16 and 17. Bn. Centres went off at once to reconnoitre line and Bn. moved off about 10.30 p.m. The 88th Inf. Bde. had only occupied the posts for 14 hours and so the battalion was relieving 3 regiments	
BAILLEUL	do 15(?)	am 5.30	relief was not completed until 5.20 am. Bn. dug themselves in as follows, having acc/from corps holding line advances pob - 1 from each coy. These tob wire dug in on forward slopes along the line S.21.d.01 to S.23.6.0.0. distributed at intervals about 400". They were each garrisoned by 1 Platoon. Each coy held in rt. part of the support line with 3 platoons. The line was dug on the reverse slopes of the REVELSBURG RIDGE along the line S.21.d 0.5 to S.23.a.7.5. Bn. H.Q. in a trench at S.16.c.0.7.	
— do —	do	6.0 am	Two hostile patrols about 30 strong advanced against our post in S.22.d. They were driven off leaving 3 prisoners in our hands and 17 dead + wounded in front of our post.	
		7.0 am	A hostile patrol advanced against a M.G. post in S.22.c. They were counter attacked and driven off, leaving 12 prisoners in our hands.	
		12.0 noon	During the morning 3 deserters came over to our lines. For an account of the operations during the remainder of the day see Special appendix attached.	
— do —	16/4/18	2.0 am	Brit. 4th withdrew n/ther through the 34th Division positions in S.10.c and d and moved to LOCRE where they were joined by details from companies who took dress to BAILLEUL	JCW
LOCRE	17/4/18	5.0 am	Bn. was arranged into two companies with a Lewis gun and rested all day. The composite battalion then	

Army Form C. 2118.

WAR DIARY
or
INTELLIGENCE SUMMARY.
(Erase heading not required.)

Ref. to FRANCE Sheet 2 E.S.W. 20000

Place	Date	Hour	Summary of Events and Information	Remarks and references to Appendices
LOCRE	17/4/18		Formed was known as Major HOLMES' Bn after commander of 4th Lincolns K.1774. Bde until detail attached was known as General JAMES' FORCE.	
		8.30 a.m.	Bn moved up to position of readiness for counter attack at opport. to front line in area M.29 a. and C. According to orders Coys were dug in in and about the wood in M.29 c. but heavy enemy shelling forced the evacuation of the wood. Boys then dug in in narrow sts in M.29 a. 2nd Lieut. J. FISHER was killed and 2nd Lieut. V. du PLERGNY seriously wounded. Subsequently dying at the C.C.S. 15 or more killed and wounded. Bn remained in position all day.	
—do—		10.0 p.m.	Bn with drew to camp at LOCRE M.17 c. 2.2	
	18/4/18	8.0 a.m.	Bn moved to assembly position in M.29 remaining all day entirely without casualties. Withdrawing to camp at M.17 e.2.2. at 9.30 p.m.	
	19/4/18	9.0 a.m.	Bn moved to assembly position in M.29. remaining all day.	
		11.0 p.m.	Bn was relieved by a company of the 51st Regiment 34th French Division Bn on relief moved to RENINGHELST	
RENINGHELST	20/4/18	12.0 noon	Bn moved by march route to a camp in A.30 arriving about 2.30 p.m.	
BRANDHOEK	21/4/18	9.0 a.m.	Bn moved by march route to HOUTKERKE and was accommodated in farms at D.6.d.2.7 and D.18.c.2.7.	
HOUTKERQUE	21/4/18 to 25/4/18		Training Mitens Sewers and bombers continued. All companies carried out close order drill. for respirator drill. Lewis gunners and musketry daily.	

Army Form C. 2118.

WAR DIARY
or
INTELLIGENCE SUMMARY.

(Erase heading not required.)

Instructions regarding War Diaries and Intelligence Summaries are contained in F. S. Regs., Part II. and the Staff Manual respectively. Title pages will be prepared in manuscript.

Ref: French Belgium Sheet 27 and 28

Place	Date	Hour	Summary of Events and Information	Remarks and references to Appendices
HOUTKERQUE	26/4/18	3.0 pm 5.30 pm	Bn was ordered to be ready to move at short notice. Orders received to embus at HOUTKERQUE for St. JAN. TER. BIEZEN where new huts carried out the Battalion being accommodated in Scheve Camp in L.3.c (Sheet 27)	
St JAN-ter-BIEZEN	27/4/18	5.0 pm	Bn moves to relieve the 11th Suffolk Regt in the E. POPERINGHE line another DUDGEDOM Switch. This was completed at 11.30 pm. Another Bn disposed as follows (Ref to Sheet 28 N.E) E POPERINGHE line. Right Coy (D. Coy) from G.3.d.F.5. to G.33.c.8.0. in support at G.33.d.F.5. Coy HQ G.32.d.9.7. This Coy had an advanced Lewis Gun Post at G.33.c.2.0. Left Coy (A Coy) from G.33.c.3.9 to junction with 4 Leicesters at G.33.a.2.5. with a platoon in support at G.32.b.9.5. Right Coy (C. Coy) from G.33.a.4.2 to G.33.b.2.4. Left Coy (B.Coy) from G.33.b.2.4 to G.34.a.2.9. having HQ 2/6 B. OUDERDOM Switch Staffords on the left made continuation Etc Bristol Bn H.Q. farm at G.32.a.4.7.	
RENINGHELST	28/4/18	6.0 pm	Front line is in region of LOCRE. Shelled by 154th and 39th Trench Mortar Batteries are now in an active state during the day. Enemy artillery moderate after. A. Coy returns with the E POPERINGHE line by the 4th Leicester Regt. Bn front is now – POPERINGHE line G.32.d.5.0 to G.33.a.4.2. Switch line as before. A Coy moved to Bn HQ Becomes reserve Coy.	
-do-	29/4/18	3.00 am	Heavy bombardment by enemy during the morning. Our Guns reply). Late information as shows that Germans attacked the Scherpenberg and MONTROUGE on our front and penetrated line to about M.17 central. The French line was subsequently found to extend 3 way bombardment we suffered a few casualties a few casualties to T.R.	

D. D. & L., London, E.C. (A8004) Wt. W1771/M2 31 759,000 5/17 Sch. 52 Forms/C2118/14

Army Form C. 2118.

Instructions regarding War Diaries and Intelligence
Summaries are contained in F. S. Regs., Part II.
and the Staff Manual respectively. Title pages
will be prepared in manuscript.

Ref June Sheet 28. N.W.

WAR DIARY
or
INTELLIGENCE SUMMARY.
(Erase heading not required.)

Place	Date	Hour	Summary of Events and Information	Remarks and references to Appendices
RENINGHELST	29/4/15	—	A Coy moved one platoon to support B Coy in Voordom Street. Taking up posts at G.33.6.5.8. The remainder 2 B Coy became forward reserve and occupied trench at G.33.a.8.9.	
— do —	30/4/15	—	Dispositions unchanged. Heavy artillery action shelling our own & enemy the whole morning.	
do.		6.30 pm	Trench attacked enemy position - movement known.	

Army Form C. 2118.

WAR DIARY
or
INTELLIGENCE SUMMARY.
(Erase heading not required.)

Place	Date	Hour	Summary of Events and Information	Remarks and references to Appendices
KEMMINGHELST	30/4/18		The following officers have joined during the month. Lieut A.B. HARDY. Capt. J.S. NICHOLLS. Lieut M. BAMBER. Lieut P.D. BROOK. Lieut G.V. DARBY " W.G. FENTON ; Lieut P.W. HALLIDAY. Lieut N. COLICER " O. DAVIES " J.W. NUTTALL " W.V. Du PLERGNY. Lieut L.G. DICKINSON. " PATERSON " J. FISHER " CLOUGH. Capt. MRO MANNING Capt. A.C. WALLIS. Wounds, NIMMO, MESSUM, DEANE, from the S. Lancs Regt. The following officers have been struck off during the month. Lieut Colonel H.B. ROFFEY. D.S.O. Killed in action 15/4/18. Lieut L.G. DICKINSON. wounded do " W.G. FENTON missing do " J.C. MYERS. do do " J. FISHER. Killed in action 17/4/18 " V.W. du PLERGNY died of wounds " do.	

1/5/18

J Ainscow Major
Cmdg 9/5th Lincolnshire Regt

2/5 Lincoln Regt Order No 70
Ref FRANCE Sheet 28.   9.4.18

1. The Bn will be relieved in the front line trenches of the left sub sector by the 4th Leicester Regt tomorrow 10/4/18.

2. D Coy 4th Leic Regt will relieve D Coy 2/5 Lincs Regt
   C   "   "   "   "   "   C   "   "   "
   B   "   "   "   "   "   A   "   "   "
   A   "   "   "   "   "   B   "   "   "

3. Guides will be provided as under reporting to Bn HQ at 4.0 p.m.
   D & C. 1 guide per platoon (4) & 1 for Coy H.Q.
   A & B. 1 guide for each 2 platoons & 1 for Coy H.Q.
   H.Q. Bn. 1 guide.

4. Reliefs of all posts except front line will be carried out by daylight unless visibility is too good.

5. A. C & D Coys with Bn HQs will, on relief, move to St Jean Camp. Q.M. will arrange guides to be at Cross Roads I.4.a.3.0. to meet Coys & guide to Camp. Q.M. will take over St Jean Camp from 4th Leic during morning 10/4/18.
   B. Coy on relief will occupy posts of the Divisional Reserve line relieving a Coy of the 4th Leicester. O/C B will apply to adjt for details.

6. All defence schemes, maps, plans &c will be handed over. Separate receipts will be handed over today for reserve rations water & S.a.a. &c. Trench stores will be

handed over including hot food containers (petrol tin pattern also) and all petrol tins, dixies will be handed over, & receipts will be forwarded to HQ by 6.0 p.m. 11/4/18. Representatives of 4 Lin Regt will arrive early tomorrow to take over.

7. Transport officer will arrange Transport as under :- 1 Limber per Coy to be at ration dump at dusk.

   1 Vehicle for HQ to remove Mess Stores, Officers bundles & R.A.P. & orderly Room

8. QM will arrange to deliver rations for B. Coy to the same spot as heretofore and at the same time

9. The 1 NCO & 2 men of B Coy at Bde Gum Boot Store & the 4 men of A Coy at the pumping station will be released tomorrow & will rejoin their Coys.

10. Relief complete will be wired to HQ by code words
  A Coy OVITCH
  B Coy TOLSTOI
  C Coy LENIN
  D Coy RIGA

Copy 1-5 Coys
  6 QM
  7 TO
  8 4 Lin
  9.10 War Diary
  11 File

      Capt & Adjt
      7/Lincoln Regt

An account of the part taken by the 2/5th Bn. LINCOLNSHIRE Regt in operation XIIE2 BAILLEUL on 15th April 1918.

15/4/18
12.0 noon.   At this hour the battalion was disposed as previously described in the War Diary to which this account forms an appendix. This position had been taken up during the night 14/15 Apl. 1918.

A heavy bombardment of our position commenced at 12.0 noon when & continued until 2.30 pm when it changed to a barrage falling along our line and that of the units on our right and left.

2.45 pm.   The enemy delivered an attack against the 4th LINCOLN Regt on our left but their line remained intact.

3.40 pm.   Enemy attack developed against our right company in S 21 d. This attack was repulsed by our Lewis gun and rifle fire.

4.30 pm.   Left Coy Cmdr reported the enemy on the ridge on his immediate left and that the 4th Lincolns had fallen back from the ridge. They formed a defensive flank facing E, still keeping touch with our left Coy (D. Coy)

5.25 pm At 6.25 pm the line of the 4th Lincoln Regt in S.16.b and 17a withdrew to the railway cutting in S.17a, 11c, 16b and 16a

5.45 pm The enemy forced his way over the neck of the hill at S.16d, breaking the line of the 4th Lincolns and getting behind the left flank of our battalion, including one platoon of the 4th Lincolns which had continuously maintained touch with our left.

At the same time a frontal attack developed along our front. The left Coy was last seen in its original positions fighting at very close quarters with the enemy. The Lewis guns of this company fired to the last at the enemy advancing in close formations, at very short range. The remaining 3 companies on the ridge came under very heavy machine gun fire from the left where the enemy had gained a footing on the ridge. These companies had heavy casualties and swung round to form a flank facing E. They were gradually driven back on to a line taken up by the 176 Infy Bde N.E. of BAILLEUL

6.15 pm Patrols were sent out from Bn HQ to get in touch with the companies in front but found only the enemy. To conform with the movements of the 4th LINCOLN Rgt Bn H.Q. withdrew to S.10.c.7.2. where 2 coys of the 9th Northumberland Fusiliers were found to be holding a line. The Bn H.Q. personnel were organised into fire units and extended the line of the Fusiliers to

7.0pm: the right, from S.10.c.3.2 to S.10.c.7.2. The enemy attack was checked here. During the night the enemy by means of patrols pushed forward on finding that our right flank was open. Several patrols were sent out to try and establish touch with our troops on the right but without success. In order to prevent the enemy penetrating this gap, 2 platoons of the 9th N. Fusiliers were brought up and the line extended some 500" to the N.W. to S.9.d.90.75. This was

11.0pm. the position when orders were received from Bde to withdraw to LOCRE.

The following casualties were sustained:
Killed. Lieut Colonel. H. B. ROFFEY. D.S.O.
~~Died of wounds. 2Lieut V. — de PIERCEY.~~
Wounded. " L. G. DICKINSON.
Missing. " W. G. FENTON, 2nd/Lieut. J. C. MYERS
OR Killed, wounded & missing. 352.

19.4.18

J Anderson Major
Ag O/C Lincoln Rgt

Operation Order No. 69.
7.5 pm when Ref.

1. The Bn will relieve the 9th Bn H.L.I. in the left sub sector of 100th Bde front tonight.
2. D Coy will take over right front line.
   C " " " left "
   A " " " support
   B " " " reserve.
3. Guides as under will meet Coys at BORRY FARM.
   1 per platoon
   1 " Coy HQ
   1 " Bn HQ
   The Adjutant will be at BORRY FARM to allot guides.
4. Battn will move up by trains from QUINTIN Station G.7.b.7.0. as follows:
   1st train. 50 of C. Coy train leaves 6.45 pm
   2nd   "   remainder of C. Coy
              D Coy   } — 7.0 pm
              A "
              B "
   3rd   "   Bn H.Q.   — 7.15 pm
   Troops will arrive 15 mins before train times. Time of marching out of camp will be notified.
5. 1 Blanket per man will be carried by A & B Coys.

2/5 Lincoln Regt.   Order No. 68

1. The Battn will entrain tomorrow at HOUDAIN for PROVEN
2. Billeting party as under will report to Staff Captain at 11.45 am at HOUDAIN Station ready to proceed by 12 noon train:
    2/Lt E.G.V. RIGHTON
    Interpreter Lefebvre
    1 NCO for H.Q. and each Coy
   A lorry will convey party from PROVEN to Billets.
3. Bn will parade at HQ at 11.40 am Dress: F.S.M.O. carrying 1 blanket per man & rations for consumption tomorrow. Discis will be taken. Any surplus baggage must be dumped at Station 2 hrs before train time with loading party. Q.M. will report what baggage requires to be moved
4. 2/Lt E.A. DENNIS will reconnoitre approaches to Station & guide Bn in. He will report to RTO at 11.45 am for instructions & will be in possession of entraining state.

31.7.18.
Capt & Adjt
2/5 Lincoln Regt

Tomorrow's rations & filled water bottles will be carried by all men. Water & biscuits will be delivered by A.M. to ration dumps tonight. Other administrative arrangements will be notified.

6. Dispositions in line will be reported to Bn H.Q. by 6.0 p.m. tomorrow 5/4/18.
7. Transport arrangements have been notified.
8. Camp must be left thoroughly clean & tidy.
9. Relief complete will be notified to Bn H.Q. by Code word HAPPY.

4/4/18

Capt & Adjt
7th Lincolns Regt

Confidential

Vol 16

21/30

WAR DIARY
of the
2/5th Bn. LINCOLN: Regt.
For the
Month of MAY. 1918.

Army Form C. 2118.

WAR DIARY
or
INTELLIGENCE SUMMARY.
(Erase heading not required.)

CONFIDENTIAL

WAR DIARY
of the
2/5th Bn. LINCOLNSHIRE Regt
from
1/5/18
to
31/5/18

1/6/18

L.V. Barnes
Lieut. Colonel
Comdg 2/5th Lincolnshire Regt

Army Form C. 2118.

WAR DIARY
or
INTELLIGENCE SUMMARY.
(Erase heading not required.)

Ref. France Sheets 27, 28 1/40000

Place	Date	Hour	Summary of Events and Information	Remarks and references to Appendices
RENINGHELST	1/5/18 to 5/5/18		Bn remained in E. POPERINGHE LINE and OUDERDOM SOUTH. Improving the Saint proportions. Work was continued, improving and training. Enemy artillery only moderately active on our frontier and no further casualties. The French carried out several local attacks on the morning 2/5/18 and LA CLYTTE during the period.	few
— do —	5/5/18 3:0pm		Bn withdrew and marched to SHRINE CAMP, HOUTKERQUE. Lieut. Colonel E. DELME W.C. DAVIES EVANS, PEMBROKE YEOMANRY, assumed command. Major S. BOYLE BERKS Regt assumed duties of 2nd in Command.	few few
KOUTKERQUE ST. MOMELIN	6/5/18		Bn embussed and moved to SIMOMELIN (ST OMER) into beets. Preparations made for debussing each Bn enroutes are return to embussing.	
— do —	6/5/18 to 7/5/18 9/5/18		It having been decided to reduce the Battalion to a training cadre & 10 Officers and 45 OR the following were today left Julia to the Base first line transport was returned for further instructions as to its disposal. Instead E.E. BUNYAN Lieut A.A. NIMMO Major S. BOYLE. " G.V. DARBY " L.M. DEAN Capt ARO MANNING " N. COCKER Lieut A.W. MESSUM " G.V. LONGLAND " W.L. RUDALL " P.C. RENSHAW " A.B. HARDY " E.G.V. RIGHTON Lieut W.A. BALL M.C. and 490 Other Ranks	few

Army Form C. 2118.

WAR DIARY
or
INTELLIGENCE SUMMARY.
(Erase heading not required.)

Ref. *War Diaries* LENS 11

Place	Date	Hour	Summary of Events and Information	Remarks and references to Appendices
ST. MOMELIN (J. OTTER)	8/5/18		The following Offrs to proceed to Base but not available were also struck off. Lieut. M. FITZPATRICK. 2/Lieut. A.J. HEALEY 2/Lieut. L.W.M. HAWKINS. " R.T. BOARDLEY " O. DAVIES " D. PATTERSON. " " and 2/S Other ranks. Remaining with unit Lt. Colonel. D.W.C. DAVIES EVANS. 2/Capt. A.R.W. SHIRR. Capt & Adjt. J.C. URQUHART Lieut. H. BAMBER Capt. H.S. NICHOLS P.W. HALLIDAY " A.C. WALLIS Lieut. E.A. DENNIS " Major G.R. SHERWELL Lieut & QM. R.H. LEWIS. and & SI Other ranks. Also returned Lieut. A.A.F. STUBBS and 4U Oth Transport personnel finding horses	
-do-	9/5/18		Bn. with transport moved to MAMETZ into huts	
MAMETZ	10/5/18		" " " " to PRESSY into Tents.	
PRESSY-les-PERNES.	11/5/18 to		Bn. remained here. A certain amount of training was carried out. Field Troop Reading for the NCOs.	
-do-	13/5/18 14/5/18		Bn. moved incl. transport to ESTREE CAUCHIE.	
ESTREE-CAUCHIE.	15/5/18 to 27/5/18		Transport with personnel moved to Base under Lieut. A.A.F. STUBBS. Remaining with unit 7 Riding horses, 3 draught, one draught and one motor cart. Bn. training Cadre attached to 25th G.G. Bn LIVERPOOL Regt. to train and advise in Music tr.m. etc. During this time all Officers and NCOs reconducted the	

(A8004) D.D. & L., London, E.C. Wt. W1271/Ma 31 750,000 5/17 Sch. 52 Forms/C2118/14

Army Form C. 2118.

WAR DIARY
or
INTELLIGENCE SUMMARY.

(Erase heading not required.)

Ry. Pioneer Rec. 6 51 C.N.E. 36 A.S.S.

Place	Date	Hour	Summary of Events and Information	Remarks and references to Appendices
ESTREE-CAUCHIE	19/5/18 to 27/5/18		Ground between ESTREE CAUCHIE and CAPELLE FERMONT where 1 Line of Defence (B.B.Line) was to be dug and held by the 25th G.G. LIVERPOOLS in case of a break through by the enemy. Schemes were prepared providing for Battle struggles posts from the Training Cadre to collect stragglers, organise them, and attach parts into B.B. line. These parties were at W.9.A.2.B., W.15.c.22 and E.9.n.5.9. Defence Scheme was also prepared providing for the defence of the B.B. Line from the ground in W.3.c to CAMBLIGNEUL (inclusive). Two sides provided for defence of sector with 1 party Bde., 2 battalions in line and 1 in reserve. 3 hours Training was carried out daily for Training Cadre in Close order Drill, Physical Training and Bayonet fighting, and Lewis Gun. Bn. entrained at TINQUES for ALLERY (France) near DIEPPE 16). Tunnels were cut carried to ABBEVILLE from where Bn. marched to ALLERY and went into billets on 29/5/18.	
— do —	29/5/18		Bn. now a part of 21st Qty. Relay, 30th Division and on the instructions to the 66th Bty. Bde. U.S. Army for forwarding to instructions. The following were attached to each American Battalion for instructional purposes. 1 Company Commander 1 C.S.M. 1 Sec. NCO 1 Musketry Instructor 1 Lewis Gun Instructor	
ALLERY (DIEPPE. 16.)	29/5/18 to 31/5/18		Remainder of the Bn. Training Cadre until the attacks to the M.O. of the 132nd Infy. Regt. to assist and instruct.	

Bn/Brig Lieut Col. O/C 2/Bn Lincoln R M.E.F.

Army Form C. 2118.

WAR DIARY
or
INTELLIGENCE SUMMARY.
(Erase heading not required.)

WO 95/3028

YB 17

CONFIDENTIAL

WAR DIARY

of the
2/5th Bn. The Lincolnshire Regiment

from
1/6/18 to 30/9/18

John Davis
Lieut Colonel
Comdg 2/5th Lincolnshire Regt

1/7/18

Army Form C. 2118.

WAR DIARY
or
INTELLIGENCE SUMMARY.

(Erase heading not required.)

Ref France Sheets { DIEPPE / ABBEVILLE / AMIENS / LENS }

Instructions regarding War Diaries and Intelligence Summaries are contained in F. S. Regs., Part II. and the Staff Manual respectively. Title pages will be prepared in manuscript.

Place	Date	Hour	Summary of Events and Information	Remarks and references to Appendices
ALLERY	1/6/18 to 10/6/18		Bn. still existing as a training Cadre & instructional purpose. A Company Commander was attached to 132nd Regt American Infantry for training purposes to American Regt 119. Chief work musketry (including British Rifle & Lewis Gun) Tactical exercises without troops were also frequently carried out. 132nd Regt American Infantry Off Allery.	
	10/6/18 to 11/6/18		Tactical schemes without troops were carried out each day under Bde. Command.	Yes
MONCHAUX	12/6/18		Bn. proceeded to MONCHAUX where similar training was continued	
Ch'du de la HME	15/6/18 to		Bn. proceeded to Chateau de la HME (near GAMACHE) adjoining the 132nd Regt American Infantry. Training was continued. One company cadre was allotted to each company of American Infy (No 1 Bn) and Bn HQ remains attached to 132nd Regt HQ. Training in musketry, L.G. Tactical exercises Range practice & Inspection.	Yes
MOLLIENS au BOIS	20/6/18 to		Bn. moved by Lorry to MOLLIENS au BOIS with 132nd Regt Am Infy. Training was continued. Attention being paid to rifle & Lewis Gun. During the time reserve lines & trenches were reconnoitred by Amn Officers and the troops spent one night in a reserve system preparing the routine of ordinary trench warfare. Bn transferred to 193 Bde 60 Div on 21.6.18	Yes Yes
BERTEAUCOURT (LENS 10)	27/6/18 to 26/6/18		Bn marched to BERTEAUCOURT staying one night and another next am to BERTEAUCOURT for attachment to 3rd Bn. (30th American Infantry. Bn Comdr administration. Training	
MONFLIERS (ABBEVILLE)	30/6/18		MONFLIERS, 199th Inf Bde US Division for command now under 199th U/S Bde US Division for command of American troops continued - musketry rifle Lewis Gun wh grenade, Bn drill p.t. & f.t. & field subjects	Yes

Army Form C. 2118.

WAR DIARY
or
INTELLIGENCE SUMMARY.
(Erase heading not required.)

Place	Date	Hour	Summary of Events and Information	Remarks and references to Appendices
MONFLIERS	30/6/18	—	The following Officer left the Bn on Transfer to S. LANCS Regt. Capt A C WALLIS. Mentioned in dispatches (London Gaz 24/5/18.) 2/Lieut (A/Capt) A R W SKIPP. do 3/6/18.) Capt J E URQUHART. Awarded M.C.	

17/7/18

John Davies Esqr
Lieut. Colonel
Cmdg 2/5th Bn Kinrok Regt

2/5 Bn Lincolnshire Regt.
Operation Order No. 127   12/6/18

1. The Batn will move today from this area to MONCHAUX.
2. Route - OISEMONT - RAMBURES - BOUTTENCOURT - MONCHAUX.
3. Starting Point. Head of column will be at cross roads 300 yds. N. of railway crossing, ready to move off at 3 p.m.
4. Dress. F.S.M.O.
5. Baggage. All baggage, officers valises, etc will be at wagon lines by 2pm. The Comdg Officer will see the wagons loaded at that time.
6. Billets. All billets, wagon lines, etc will be left in a scrupulously clean condition. Lt A. Barnaby has proceeded to billet in the new area.

Capt & Adjt
2/5 Lincoln Regt

2/5 Lincoln Regt
Operation Order No. 29   14/6/18

1. The Bn will move tomorrow to LA HAIE CAMP via GAMACHE station & will relieve the detachment of the Manchester Regt.

2. Bn will parade at 2 pm. Head of column 100x West of railway crossing.

3. Lt Rambas & C.Q.M.S Herne will report to the detachment of 17 Manchester Regt & make themselves acquainted with all the billets. They will proceed on bicycles, leaving MONCHAUX at 11 am

4. The G.S. Wagons will call for Officers Mess Kits & all Baggage at 1 pm. which must be ready for loading before that hour.

5. Dress. F.S.M.O.

14/6/18   Capt & Adjt
                           2/5 Lincoln Regt

Army Form C. 2118.

WAR DIARY
or
INTELLIGENCE SUMMARY.
(Erase heading not required.)

WB 14

CONFIDENTIAL.

War Diary of the 75th Bn
The Lincolnshire Regt
from
1/7/15 to 31/7/15

J. Christopher Capt
Cmdg 2/5 Lincoln Regt
1/8/15

Army Form C. 2118.

WAR DIARY
or
INTELLIGENCE SUMMARY.
(Erase heading not required.)

Ref: France Sherwin Lewis Abercorn Diary

Instructions regarding War Diaries and Intelligence Summaries are contained in F. S. Regs., Part II. and the Staff Manual respectively. Title pages will be prepared in manuscript.

Place	Date	Hour	Summary of Events and Information	Remarks and references to Appendices
MONFLIERS (Abbeville)	1/7/18	—	Battalion training staff attached to 130 American Infy Regt for training purposes	—
RIBEAUCOURT (new in)	3/7/18	—	Marched to RIBEAUCOURT.	—
Le SOUICH	4/7/18	—	Marches to Le SOUICH for attachment to 2 & 3rd Bns 319th Am Infantry Regt	—
- do -	4/7/18 to 20/7/18	—	Assisting with training & administration of American units also	—
CANDAS	21/7/18	—	Marches to CANDAS.	—
- do -	22/7/18	—	A/Capt (Lieut) G.R. SHERWELL posted to 1st Bn LINCOLNSHIRE Regt.	—
- do -	do.	—	Entrained at CANDAS for SERQUEUX.	—
ABANCOURT	29/7/18	—	Marches to camp near ABANCOURT awaiting orders for disbandment	—
- do -	31/7/18	—	Battalion disbanded. Other ranks posted to 1/5 Bn LINCOLNSHIRE Regt.	—
			Officers awaiting postings	
			Lieut Col. D.W.E. DAVIES EVANS Capt H.S. NICHOLS	
			Capt r/a/Lt J.C. URQUHART. Lieut P.W. HALLIDAY.	
			Lieut M.W. SICH P.P. " H. CAMBER	
			Lt/Qn. R.H. LEWIS. " F.A. DENNIS	

FINIS

1/8/18

JC Urquhart Capt
Cmdg 2/5 Lincolnshire Regt

www.ingramcontent.com/pod-product-compliance
Lightning Source LLC
Chambersburg PA
CBHW081407160426
43193CB00013B/2126